Alone in Vietnam

Red Dog Books
P.O. Box 1242
Glastonbury, Ct 06033
1-866-766-2253-
E-mail 424219@comcast.net

Editors
Eileen Stanley
Thomas E. Michaels
Colette Weber

Red Dog Books, P.O. Box 1242 Glastonbury, CT 06033 or call 1-866-766-2253
e-mail 424219@comcast.net

TO ORDER MORE BOOKS CALL 1-866-766-2253
OR
SEE OUR WEB PAGE AT:
http://www.independentpublisher-us.com:80/aloneinvietnam.htm

Although the author and publisher have made every effort to ensure the accuracy and completeness of information contained in this book, we assume no responsibility for errors, inaccuracies, omissions, or any inconsistency here in. Any slights of people, places, or organizations are unintentional. First printing 2007.

Attn: corporations, universities, colleges, and professional organizations: quantity discounts are available on bulk purchases of this book for educational, give purposes, or as premiums for increasing magazine subscriptions or renewals, special books or book and Serbs can also be created to fit specific needs. For information, please contact my publishing company,
Red Dog Books, P.O. Box 1242, Glastonbury, CT 06033 or call 1-866-766-2253
E-mail 424219@comcast.net

Alone in Vietnam

Tour of Duty in South Vietnam
June 3, 1968–June 3, 1969

United States Army
Americal Division
196th Light Infantry Brigade
Third Battalion of the Twenty-first Infantry
Regiment
Company D, "Black Death"
Second Platoon
Second Rifle Squad, June–August 1968
Machine Gun Squad, September 1968–June 1969

Robert B. Boyd Jr.

2008

Alone in Vietnam

TABLE OF CONTENTS

This is the type of letter I got In December, 1967

This book is dedicated to my wife,
Arline M. Boyd,
Who has been putting up with these stories for 30 years.

PREFACE

This book is a narrative account of the events that happened to me as a twenty-year-old draftee from Connecticut in 1968.

The title "Alone in Vietnam" refers to the United States Army's policy of a 365-day tour of duty in Vietnam, which was in effect at the time. By setting a separate date for each soldier to go home, the Army unwittingly set up a target date—a goal for each soldier to try to reach. That goal was to try to survive until his day to go home.

Because of this system of everyone having his own countdown until he went home, it made you feel you were "Alone in Vietnam."

These are my stories: They are true, not moral

I make no apologies. There are no happy endings

These are my stories

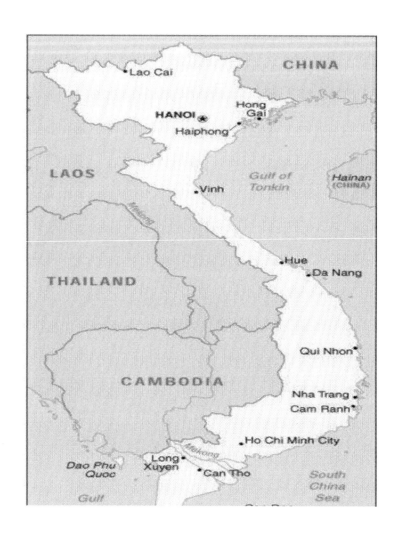

INTRODUCTION TO THE VIETNAM WAR

The Vietnam War was a war fought between 1964 and 1975 on the ground in South Vietnam and bordering areas of Cambodia and Laos, and in bombing runs over North Vietnam.

Fighting on one side was a coalition of forces including the United States, the Republic of Vietnam, Australia, New Zealand, and South Korea.

Fighting on the other side was a coalition of forces including the Democratic Republic of Vietnam (North Vietnam) and the National Liberation Front, a communist-led South Vietnamese guerrilla movement.

The USSR provided military aid to the North Vietnamese and to the NLF (Viet Cong), but was not one of the military combatants.

PART I

INDUCTION DAY

Induction was abrupt. After filling out some forms and answering a few questions, the swearing-in ceremony took place. We all raised our hands and swore to God something about protecting our country, and we were in the Army.

The person in charge, a PFC (Private First Class), got everybody's attention and asked us, "How long have you just been drafted for? How many years from today do you have to spend in the Army?" He seemed to like asking this question. He conducted this induction ceremony every day, and from the way he acted, I could see he took pleasure in asking this question of every group. I could tell I was not going to like the answer.

After we all yelled out, "Two years," because everybody knew if you got drafted you were in the Army for two years, his answer was, "Six years. Your military obligation is six years. Everybody in this room who just took the oath will be in the United States Army for a period of not less than six years." It sounded like a sentence—for a lot of us, a death sentence. My first thought was, "Boy, is my mother going to be mad. I told her I would only have to be in for two years." As it turned out, he was right. After two years, draftees who served in Vietnam were relieved of active duty and reassigned to an inactive reserve unit for four years. If you didn't go to Vietnam, you were assigned to an active reserve unit and did your weekends and two weeks in the summer for four years. Either way, nobody in that room got his discharge any sooner than six years.

Well, some got their discharge sooner—dishonorable discharges and medical discharges took less time. Of course, if you were killed in Vietnam you got out sooner, but I don't think he was counting that.

PART II

BASIC TRAINING

Fort Dix in January 1968 was cold and scary. We learned all that Army stuff—marching, saluting, basic weapons skills—and got into pretty good physical shape. Basic training was for everybody: guys joining the National Guard, who would get to go home after basic; men earmarked for specific jobs because of their civilian education; and professional civilians—lawyer types.

I met all types of men, from recent Yale graduates to guys who worked on the docks of New York City as longshoremen. We all had a common interest though, getting through each day as best we could until basic training was over. We all knew we were in the Army, but we also knew a lot of guys in the Army didn't go to Vietnam, even in 1968. And a lot of guys who did go to Vietnam were not in the infantry, not combatants. In Vietnam, for every sorry ass who ended up in the infantry there were seven support personnel in the rear, doing jobs that were not directly in combat.

The United States Army had a lot of troops in South Korea, and a lot in Germany and the rest of Europe, so you had a good chance of not going to Vietnam at all, or so you told yourself. Even if you got orders to go to Vietnam, most Army personnel in Vietnam weren't in the infantry, wading around in rice paddies and killing gooks (derogatory term for an Asian). It all depended on your MOS (Military Occupational Specialty), your job title. Your whole military experience would be based on your MOS. If your MOS said you were a cook, you were sent to cooking school and you cooked. If your MOS said you were a truck driver, you went to truck-driving school and drove a truck.

When basic training was over, we had a graduation ceremony. Bands played and there were speakers. Some guys even had their families come and watch as we marched by the reviewing stand with our new bodies and our nice dress uniforms.

After graduation, we got our orders. I looked at mine and of course didn't have any idea what they said—Army jargon. There was a small group of guys standing around one of the drill sergeants, asking him to explain their orders for them. When it was my turn to show him my orders, he read them and looked up with real compassion. He said, "I am sorry son. You're an IIB IO. You're in the infantry; you are going to Tiger Land for AIT (Advanced Infantry Training)." I thought, "What the hell is Tiger Land?" Up until that moment, that sergeant had been the meanest person I had ever met. In three months of being in his presence every day, I had never heard anything come out of his mouth that wasn't loud, crude, or demeaning. When he spoke to me in such a kind way, I felt a cold hand on my shoulder. I shivered.

Later that day everyone was talking, saying how happy they were that basic was over, where they were going for training, and wishing each other good luck. When I told my friends what my orders were, I started to get "the look." This is where the separation started. This is where the "us" and "them" started. I wasn't sure if I was an "us," or a "them," but I was sure there was no more "we."

"………. Abandon every hope, ye who enter here."

Inscription on the gate to Hell in the book
"Dante's *Inferno*"

PART III

TIGER LAND

I arrived in Fort Polk, Louisiana, by bus in a few days. We IIB I0s had been joined on the way by other IIB I0s and were all now seated on two buses—in the Deep South, sitting on buses without air conditioning, sitting in a parking lot waiting to go to our new barracks to start our advanced infantry training. As we waited, some guys got off the bus and smoked a cigarette. We could see the bus driver talking to some officer, probably about where he should take us. All of a sudden some sergeant came running over to the buses, shouting to the guys standing around outside to get back in the bus. "You can't get off that bus! You're going to Tiger Land!"

Tiger Land. We had no idea what Tiger Land was, but the way the name was used made it sound like a threat or a curse, like, "You're going to a leper colony." The sergeant acted like they had committed some crime by just touching the ground, like they were exposing the rest of the fort to some disgusting disease that wasn't talked about in decent company. As it turned out, Tiger Land was for the cursed, a place decent people didn't go to or even talk about.

Tiger Land was a large training camp isolated inside Fort Polk, a United States Army base located on 198,000 acres in western Louisiana. The whole area was nasty swamp land, and Tiger Land was located in the biggest, most bug-infested swamp on the base. This was the Louisiana bayou, Cajun country. To a New England Yankee like me, it might as well have been the moon.

The buses drove on for another half hour, going on smaller and smaller roads, with the swamp growing larger and deeper on both sides. It became darker and muggier until we came to a guard station with armed guards, a high chain-linked fence, and a closed gate. A sergeant had gotten on each bus and rode standing up by the bus door. Ours was the first bus and when it stopped at the gate the newcomer got out and talked to the guard, and the guard raised the gate to let us through. I will never forget the large sign over the gate, "TIGER LAND," and a smaller sign on the side that said, "Welcome to little Vietnam." We got off the buses and were quickly assembled and marched to a pre-fabricated one-story building. Above the door was a sign saying, "Tiger Land Orientation Center." We were marched inside and seated in chairs and we waited. You do a lot of waiting in the Army.

We sat in our chairs facing a low stage with a podium in the middle, and quietly waited for the speaker to come out and start our orientation. All of a sudden, a man came running out from the right side of the stage screaming and firing a rifle as he went into a kneeling position. His face was darkened with camo stick and he wore strange fatigues. When he was done firing, he jumped up and threw the M-16 rifle he was holding through the air like a spear. It had a bayonet fixed to the muzzle and it stuck into a large wooden bench that was leaning against the wall about twenty feet away. It made a twanging sound, and the room was silent.

The commander of Tiger Land, some colonel, stormed onto the stage and stood at the podium. "Gentlemen, that was to get your attention." He paused, took a slow look around the room and said, "Every man in this room will be in Vietnam in one hundred twenty days as an infantry soldier." There it was. I wasn't going to be a cook, and I wasn't going to be a truck driver. I was going to the rice paddies. I got a sharp pain in my chest and realized I had stopped breathing.

It's not like I was that surprised, but to come out with it like that—one hundred twenty days. The colonel said everybody should go outside and take a deep breath and think about what he just said, and then come back inside so we could get to work. I remember standing outside smoking a cigarette with a guy I was with in basic, a short guy from New Jersey. We both kept shifting our feet, trying not to look at each other. I wanted to say something but couldn't get the words out. Instead, we kept looking at each other and then looking back at the ground. That cold hand that made me shiver in Fort Dix, when I first heard of Tiger Land, now gripped my heart and squeezed.

Back inside, the colonel explained what Tiger Land was. It was the main training area for the United States Army's jungle infantry training, specifically designed for ground troops going to Vietnam. It was chosen because of its location, having swamps and snakes and such, like in Vietnam. This was where the special arms training and tactics would be taught. The instructors were hand picked and they were the best in the Army. All the instructors, including our drill sergeants, had served at least one tour in the real Tiger Land, nickname for Vietnam, and he assured us they would make our stay as unpleasant as possible. We were told we could not leave the compound for weekend leaves for the first three weeks and then we were not to go anywhere on the Fort Polk base. We would be escorted out on buses and brought to the local town, Leesville. It seemed the regular base was off limits to us—more of that "us" and "them" stuff.

The physical training was very hard. We marched a lot, and it was hot. The classes were surprisingly well done and informative. The instructors treated us with respect and really seemed to want to help us learn. A typical day was spent running or marching or doing exercise, with classes in grenade throwing or spotting booby traps on the trail sprinkled in throughout the day. The big test at the end was a night infiltration course and a raid on a Viet Cong (the Communist-led forces fighting the South Vietnamese government) village the next day.

Finally the third week came, and we were all getting weekend passes. On this Saturday morning we assembled on the company compound about 11:30. The CO (Commanding Officer) came out of his office to address the company. He was a short, nasty prick who rarely spoke, and when he did speak his voice was a hiss, sort of vicious, not like a drill sergeant's bark. When he yelled at you it was real personal, like he knew you when you were kids and hated you. He was only about twenty-three years old and he kind of limped when he walked out to address us. His face was scarred, too. I thought that might be why he was so mean.

I don't remember his exact words but it went something like this: "Gentlemen, you have one hundred days from today until your plane lands in Vietnam. Look at the man to your right and then look at the man to your left. Those men will die in Vietnám. When you get to Vietnam you will take the place of some other man who has been killed or seriously wounded. You will stay and fight with that unit until you are killed or seriously wounded, and then somebody else that we train here will take your place. That is your lot in life. That outcome cannot be changed.

"What can be changed, however, is how you spend these next one hundred days, when you are not in training. You don't have the luxury that Jody has (Jody is Army jargon for the guy back home who got out of the draft—the guy with the college deferment or the flat feet). Jody can take life easy, scope out the babes, slowly get to know a woman and make his move when the time is right. You have one hundred days to do all your living and loving, and I suggest you start by going to town and getting drunk—as drunk as you can. You men don't have time for social drinking, and I don't want to hear any crap about 'I don't drink,' because if you don't you better start. Do everything you ever wanted to do in your life in the next one hundred days because for most of you, that's all you have.

"And for those of you that do make it back, I can assure you, from personal experience, that pretty young American girls are not attracted to gimps with facial disfigurements." With that last remark he gestured toward his own crippled leg and face. I have never heard such a warm and caring speech from anyone in my life. For this man to expose himself, with the reference to his physical disabilities, showed me that despite his usual demeanor he really cared about us and was giving us the best advice he could.

The following week he said the same thing, with ninety-three days left, but with a new twist. He said that it had come to his attention that some men were not going to town but were staying in the barracks, to save money. They were sending money home to their families. He explained that their families would collect plenty of money from their $10,000 government life insurance policy when Charlie (the enemy Viet Cong) killed them. He said he couldn't make them go to town and get drunk and sleep with women, but he was going to personally inspect the barracks all weekend long, and if he caught anyone there trying to save a few bucks to send home to mama, they would be digging holes until Monday morning.

He said our only obligation to the Army on the weekend was to show up Monday morning at 7:00. And if we were too drunk or broke, we were to find a cab and tell the cabby to bring us to Fort Polk. He would be in the office all weekend and would send a jeep to bring us back to the company, and lend us money to pay the cab fare to the front gate. He said the money would be paid back the next payday. Being a good soldier, I obeyed his orders.

On one of these weekends I went into town with a friend of mine, I can't remember his name, from Cape Cod. Leesville was the town and there wasn't too much going on there, but they did have bars. We drank beer for about eight hours, and after we got drunk enough he confessed to me that he had been a hippie, out on the Cape. He said he had long hair and wore beads around his neck and sometimes wore flowers in his hair, like in the song. His girlfriend called him "the bare-footed boy" back on Cape Cod. So that night, after about fifty beers, he got homesick for his girlfriend and decided he wanted "Bare-footed Boy" tattooed on his stomach. He thought she would like that. I told him it sounded like a great idea. Of course, I had had about fifty beers, too. I told him if that's what he wanted, leave it up to me, his buddy, that's what I would get him. I remember we headed out of the bar to find a tattoo guy, but after that things got fuzzy.

I woke up in our barracks on Monday morning not quite remembering how things had gone. I went over to his bunk on the other side of the barracks, where he was involved in a loud argument about him throwing up into some other guy's boot. I stopped the yelling long enough to ask him about the tattoo. He looked at me and asked, "What tattoo?" Not being sure, I told him to pull up his shirt so I could see his stomach. He did and there it was, in big bold letters, "Bare-footed Boy," tattooed on his stomach. He stared at it in total bewilderment. Just then the guy whose boot he had thrown up in started up again and I thought that would be a good time for me to leave. He didn't go to town with me again.

One evening our training ended early, so I decided to go have a few beers at the beer hall. It was named Tiger Hall, of course. The crude building held about one hundred men, had some one-piece picnic tables for sitting, and stunk of stale beer. Beer was served in plastic pitchers and poured into plastic cups. When I walked into the hall I saw it was about three-quarters full. There was a window where you bought your beer, and I started walking toward it. As I got to the window I heard noise from the center of the room and turned to see two guys standing up. Both guys seemed quite drunk and started yelling and swearing at each other. By the time I got my beer and was walking to an empty table, a fight had broken out. I sat down and watched as more people got into the fight and it started to spread like a fire. As fists were flying and bodies were being thrown over tables, I walked over to an MP (Military Police) who was sitting at a table reading a book.

I walked to a position where I could see both the MP and the fight, now getting bigger, at the same time. I asked the MP if he wasn't going to do anything to break it up. I saw he had been reading and following the fight at the same time. When I spoke to him, he carefully marked his place, closed the book, and turned to address me from a sitting position. He wore thick GI (government issued) glasses, and I noticed the book he was reading was "War and Peace." He looked at me slowly, engaging me. He seemed to be deciding if it was worth his bother to talk to me, or if he should just go back to his book. He finally spoke in an elegant, well-educated, slow southern drawl.

He said, "The United States Army didn't conceive the idea of Tiger Land, build it, staff it with its best personnel, and then put it into working operation just so some MP could stop fights when they started. The purpose of Tiger Land is to encourage fighting, bring out the trainee's aggressive nature, and let that aggressiveness blossom." He turned back to his book, dismissing me with this action. I went back to my table alone and thought about what he had said. I had seen an ambulance in the parking lot of the beer hall as I came in, and had assumed its driver had stopped in for a few beers. I now understood that the ambulance was there on standby, to take out the wounded.

The words of the MP really put the whole thing into perspective. If two men were caught fighting within our training company, they weren't disciplined for their actions like in basic training. Here they were given boxing gloves at the end of the training day and were told to fight it out, with the company of men circled around them, shouting out encouragements. I realized we were in a gladiator training camp, like in the movies. It's not like anybody was keeping it a secret. They told us this from the first day. But then I realized that like everything else in Tiger Land, the purpose of the beer hall was not for any temporary enjoyment, not for some small escape from the nonstop invasion of your body and mind. This beer hall was here to give the Army another training tool for hand-to-hand combat. For me this was my epiphany; I finally got it.

The last week of training came and we were scheduled to go through the dreaded night infiltration course and the raid on the VC (Viet Cong) village. We had all the training on how your eyes worked and how your pupils dilated when exposed to light and open again as it gets darker to let more light in so you can see in the dark. The problem, of course, is that if your eyes are already adjusted for darkness and you are exposed to light, like a trip flare going off, you are blind for all practical purposes until your eyes adjust again to the dark. By not protecting your night vision you will become vulnerable and will in all likelihood die.

This is where these instructors really showed their concern for us. They told us if we would listen to them, they would tell us how to survive long enough to come home. It was explained to us that each day in the bush was broken into two parts: daytime and nighttime. The daytime was GI time. The Viet Cong could not operate in the open during the day because of our complete control of the air. With air support for ground troops, we could go anywhere, rooting out the gooks from their hiding places and killing them. If we were outnumbered, we just called for more troops to be flown in, air mobile. If we located enemy in force, we just called in an air strike. We had observation planes in the air to tell us what the gooks were doing. Day was our time. Really, it was the Army's time.

Nighttime was referred to as "Charlie's Time" in Vietnam. All our air support went home after dark to a nice safe air base with many perimeters of protection. The grunts were left in the jungle to honker down and bear the wrath of Charlie Cong, who was coming out of his hole to go to work. His work was to find us and kill us. He was good at it, and his shift wasn't over until sun-up.

I was surprised to hear what the instructors had to say. During a typical day we would be marched through the swamps with full packs, the Louisiana heat building up, until we would come to a clearing. There was usually a small set of bleachers set up so we could all see the instructors while we sat and rested. I remember the instructors looking around as if to see if anybody was listening who could get them into trouble. They would explain to us that our mission in Vietnam was to come home in one piece. Grunts didn't get to come home because they were good at killing gooks during the day. Grunts got to come home because they were good at not getting killed at night. To understand the overall openness of that statement, that almost treasonous statement, was to understand their pleading with us to listen to their training, pay attention, so they wouldn't have more blood on their hands. Our blood.

The point was, don't worry about killing gooks. Worry about being careful, by knowing where your rifle and ammo were at night so you could find them in the dark if you were attacked. Keep a low profile, don't volunteer to go into tunnels, let someone else walk point if you can. Stay low in a firefight, let the Air Force and the artillery boys earn their pay. No one is charging you by the round; never go where a bullet could go first. The last week was their last chance to share with us all they had learned about personal survival as a grunt in Vietnam. Not the stuff in the books and manuals, but the things one grunt would share with another.

There was one last thing, one last lesson they could teach us. This lesson could not be learned from a seat in the bleachers. We couldn't learn it by reading a manual, and just telling us wouldn't make the impression on us they felt they had to, if they were going to teach us how to come home alive. The last class was in night infiltration. It was simple, really. We were all brought out to a remote area by trucks and were each given a map and a compass. About an hour before sundown we were given a briefing as to our objective.

We had to use the map and compass to travel to a point about five miles away from where we were. We could go as groups or alone, but we had to meet up at the rallying point at sunup and then conduct a raid on a Viet Cong village. In between the rallying point and us were fifty men dressed up in black pajamas to look like Viet Cong. It was their job, as mock VC, to capture us and bring us to an interrogation center located on the course. At the interrogation center we would be put in small bamboo boxes (tiger cages) and held there until our individual interrogation started. When it was our turn for interrogation, we would be taken out of the cages and brought into a room. We would be tied up and sat down in a chair and asked questions about our military strength, what secret instructions we had, and why we came here to kill innocent Vietnamese people. If we didn't respond with the answer they wanted, they would beat us with sticks.

It was pointed out to the sergeant giving the briefing that we didn't know anything; we had no information to give them. He agreed that we didn't, but said, "That fact wouldn't stop the Viet Cong from trying to force you to talk if you were captured in Vietnam, and it won't stop these mock Viet Cong from showing you how you will be treated in Vietnam if you are captured." He said, "Grunts don't go to prison camps, they are questioned and executed." He said if we were caught, these men would only speak in Vietnamese around us, except for the interrogator. He said if we were caught, we would be beaten until we lost consciousness and would be revived and beaten again. He said some of us would end up in the hospital and some would just be really bruised and sore. He said they did this exercise last in our Tiger Land training so that we wouldn't miss any training, and so we couldn't tell anybody in the classes behind us what happened, because we would be going home in a few days for our thirty-day leave. You see, the last lesson these ex-grunts, our brothers-in-arms, had to teach us was this: *Don't get caught.*

Night came and there we were, standing with our maps and compass and a full pack with water and food (C-rations) and an M-16 rifle with blanks. The sergeant who gave the briefing had left, so we were all milling around deciding who would go with whom. Some men broke up into three- or four-men teams; others like myself decided to go alone. I did not want to get captured, and from what I had seen here at Tiger Land for the last three months, that sergeant probably wasn't exaggerating—these guys were serious. If they said you would be beaten to teach you not to get captured, you would be beaten.

I looked at the topographic map. Nothing was marked on the map to show where we were or where our rallying point was. We were just given coordinates. And of course, the locations of the interrogation camp and where the mock Viet Cong would be waiting in ambush were not marked. This was Charlie Time. We were on their home ground and they had been doing this, week after week, for a long time, like the Viet Cong. I didn't know what to do, but I knew I had the whole night to do it in. I figured, what's the rush? If I did get captured, it should be as late as possible. That way the interrogators would be tired from beating everybody else who got captured and maybe they would go a little easier on me. Everybody else seemed to be in a hurry to get going—probably nerves. It's not that I was calm about the very real probability of getting the shit kicked out of me. I just thought later would be better than sooner.

I started into the woods alone. I went in about a quarter mile and sat down and ate my C-rations. I tend to eat when I am nervous, and I figured if I ate now I would have less food to carry. As it turned out, this was a good idea—not the eating part, but the sitting and waiting part. I had a lot of experience hunting and fishing in rural areas and knew my hearing was good. I sat eating with my eyes closed, listening to the night, trying to see in my mind's eye what was happening out there between our men and the mock VC.

After I finished my food I moved on, very slowly and not too far, stopping now and again to listen with my eyes closed. It was kind of like deer hunting. I didn't care how good these mock VC guys were, they weren't quieter than a deer, and at home I could hear a deer coming. I would wait motionless and listening, and when I was sure nobody was around I would move another thirty feet. The idea was to outwait the other guy; let him make a noise first by squirming or coughing, then you knew where he was and could backtrack around him.

I felt sure these mock VC wouldn't be hiding in ambush alone, so the more of them there were, the more chances someone would make a sound that I would hear. If there was one mock VC alone and he surprised me, I figured what the heck, I would beat him as hard as I could with my empty M-16. It may only have blanks in it, but I could swing it like a bat and knock the bastard out. I figured if I beat him off, he would never know who it was and I would get away scot-free. If he overwhelmed me, or his buddies came over and helped capture me, they would only do what they were going to do anyway, and I would have gotten in a few shots. I figured two could play at this game. I learned being really afraid of something could make you fearless.

I made it through the course without being captured. The interrogation compound was about halfway through the five-mile course. The camp had a bunch of thatched hooches (huts) and loud Vietnamese music was playing. The compound was lit up with bright lights and I could hear the screams of the men who had been captured. I think the ones who were caught saw the lights and heard the music and tried to get as far away from the camp as possible. This being the narrowest part of the course, all the mock VC guys had to do was wait in ambush at the point farthest from the camp and the men would come to them. I don't know for sure if this was their plan, but that's how I would do it. Instead of getting as far away from the noise and light as possible, I got as close as I could without being seen. I figured that would be the last place they would look, close to their camp. I just kept moving slowly, twenty or thirty feet at a time, stopping and listening, then moving again.

I made it to the rallying point by sunup. The ones who made it, over half, were formed into squad-size units by a drill sergeant. Each squad was given a task to do, and we raided the VC village, running, screaming, and shooting our M-16s with the blanks, and captured a bunch of mock VC.

After the night infiltration training, the AIT was over. The next day we got our orders to go on leave for thirty days and then report to a transportation unit for transfer to The Republic of South Vietnam. I didn't need anybody to explain my orders this time. They were loud and clear. I don't remember any graduation like in basic, with bands and speakers. We just got on the bus and left. The Army had to make room for the next group of 11B 10s. Our CO did remind us, though—we now had thirty days left.

PART IV

IN-COUNTRY

After a two-week, in-country training course on infantry tactics, booby traps, etc., I was assigned to a unit that did perimeter security for the Chu Lai base camp. Chu Lai was a huge camp with its own air base and was the headquarters for the American Division, the largest division in South Vietnam. It had more men, choppers, tanks, artillery, airplanes, and anything else you would need to kill the enemy. It was also located in "I Corps," the northernmost military region located on the border of North Vietnam. We were told we were quite lucky to be going to the 198th because it only pulled perimeter duty, and we wouldn't be going out to the bush much. There were about fifteen of us "green seeds" and we all crowded into the company headquarters CP (command post) room, where the top sergeant was going to assign us to our different companies.

The phone rang, something was said, and the top sergeant started to yell at us to get back on the truck. He said some infantry company in the 196th got wiped out at the DMZ (demilitarized zone) and needed replacements, so we were going there instead. The truck brought us to the rear area for the 196th, which was much smaller. It had only a small tent for the men to sleep in and a much smaller CP room. Another top sergeant was assigning us to our companies. He said we were all going to the "Black Death." That was Company D 3/21, 196th Light Infantry Brigade, American Division. The company had just come back from the DMZ and had lost most of its men, including its commanding officer, and needed a lot of replacements. I found out why the company area was so small; all the infantry companies in that battalion stayed in the field and never came back to a base camp like Chu Lai.

Just before we got back on the truck, the top sergeant gave us some last-minute advice. The item I remember best was to keep some money in our boots so that when we got hit we would be able to buy some candy and stuff in the hospital we would be sent to. Someone said, "Don't you mean *if* we get shot." The sergeant and his cronies laughed, saying, "You boys are going out to Black Death for a year. There is no way you aren't going to get hit, understand that now." When we got back on the truck I was too scared to look at anyone else.

The truck brought us to the airstrip and dropped us off. We waited there about three hours until another truck came with another group of guys that looked just like us—new uniforms, boots, helmets and helmet covers, etc. Others came until there were about forty of us, sitting on the tarmac in the open, temperature about one hundred degrees and humidity to match.

Finally a sergeant came and called out our names, and soon after that a giant Chinook helicopter landed near us. The noise was deafening. A ramp-type door dropped down in the back and two men walked out. They had helmets that covered their entire heads and faces, with black faceplates. The wind from the Chinook almost knocked us over. The sand hit our faces and bare hands and arms and stung bad. The guys from the Chinook, with the dark faceplates, had on long sleeves and gloves. They motioned us to walk up the ramp and go into the chopper. In their hands, they were holding wires that plugged into their helmets. It seemed they could talk to each other and probably to the rest of the crew. Just as the front of our two-column formation got to the ramp, they stopped us. Someone was obviously talking to them through their headsets. We stood there in full outfits—packs, weapons, etc.—as the two jet engines that powered the Chinook blew their heat out on us. I almost fainted and was starting to wobble when the column moved and I got in the chopper.

We should have stood to the side, so the heat from the turbines didn't blast us, but we didn't know better. That's when I realized nobody told you anything in Nam. You figured it out fast or died. Maybe things were discussed in the motor pool; perhaps procedure was explained in your unit orientation in any of the other thousands of jobs in the rear. In Black Death, nobody even wanted to talk to you. It was called OJT (on-the-job training).

The Chinook took us to LZ (Landing Zone) Center about forty miles southwest of Da Nang. We were assigned to our platoon by some lieutenant standing in for the company commander, who had gotten hit in the last firefight, while they were waiting for a new one to be assigned. Another guy and I were sent to a bunker where our new platoon was located. There were four guys who made up the second platoon; they looked really dirty, beaten, and distant. They never said hello, didn't ask our names, and ignored us for two days.

MY FIRST PATROL

After a few days, while new replacements came in, our platoon and another platoon went on a short patrol off the hill. At the bottom of the hill we came to the edge of a rice paddy. The sergeant who was in front of me shouted out in Vietnamese for a farmer working in the paddy to stop and come to him. The farmer, whom I had not even seen until the sergeant called out, put the hoe on her shoulder and started to walk away. I can still see the sergeant bringing his M-16 up to his shoulder, his thumb moving the selector switch to semi-auto. I could not believe he was just going to kill her. I saw his finger squeeze the trigger, as we were taught, and he blew the back of her head off.

I thought of my Catholic catechism classes, where we had to learn the Ten Commandments. *Thou shalt not kill.* I followed the sergeant over to the body. He searched her, found nothing, and motioned us to move on. I looked at his face and he didn't show any emotion, not hate, fear, disgust, or satisfaction. Just blank. That killing was never discussed by him or anyone else.

PART V

GOING INTO THE BUSH

Nobody ever told us new guys we weren't staying on the hill, that we were only there until we came up to company strength. About a week after we first got to the company, we were told by our platoon sergeant to pack up all our gear. We were going out to the field. The other new guys in the platoon and I were confused. We thought we were in the field. It was only then explained to us by one of the undead (zombies), as I thought of the old-timers. This old-timer, who had never said a word to any of us, waved his hand vaguely and said, "That is the field." What he pointed to was the vast jungle and rice paddies spread out beneath us from our view on the hill. Someone asked when we were coming back, how long the patrol was going to be. He just looked at us and said there is no coming back. You will get out of the field when your tour is up, or on a dust-off (medical evacuation chopper).

We got choppered by slicks (transport helicopters) over to LZ West and left that hill the next morning. It was the first time I had felt the weight of a fully loaded rucksack. I couldn't believe we had to carry all the gear, water, food, ammo, M-16, grenades, smoke grenades, cooking tabs, etc.

The hike down the hill took about five hours. We were now in what was called a triple-canopy jungle. It was about 11:00 A.M. and the daylight couldn't seem to get through. Even in the shade it was incredibly hot, and every bug in the jungle seemed to be biting me. We followed a stream down for another couple hours until we came to a small hill. We started up the hill and I truly was going to quit. Just when I couldn't take it anymore, we stopped for a rest. I couldn't breathe and the rucksack was digging holes in my back. When we began moving again, some gooks on top of the hill started shooting at us. There happened to be an old foxhole near me so I dropped my pack and jumped into the hole with some other guys.

The hole was large but the gooks on top of the hill had a good angle and the bullets coming into the hole were missing me by inches. I was numb with fear; I couldn't have moved if I wanted to. Just then our platoon sergeant yelled out to us, "First of the second!" That meant first squad, second platoon—us—to get on line and prepare to assault. What he was saying was that while everybody else in the company could hide, our squad had to leave our hiding place, stand shoulder to shoulder, and start running up the hill shooting our M-16s at the top of the hill. I couldn't believe he meant it. No way was I leaving the hole to go out into that rain of fire. Again I looked at his face. There was no expression, like when he killed that girl. He meant it. We got out of our hole and assaulted the hill. The gooks had left and nobody got killed. We now knew how to assault a hill. OJT.

At this point we new guys found out about PP (permanent point). The company policy was that all new guys walked point on any patrol or company movement. You got off PP when some new guy came in and took your place. I really thought they were kidding, trying to scare the new guys. They were not joking. They would get the new guys to walk out in front of everybody else, far enough so that if we hit a booby trap or tripped an ambush, the old-timer in charge wouldn't get hit. They learned this trick from the Viet Cong, who would use local women and children to walk point for them. The theory behind this policy was that if a new guy died, his life was worth less because he had suffered less. I have told this policy to a few people over the last thirty years, and each time the person would laugh, like it was a punch line to a joke. Nobody believed this could happen in the U.S. Army. I admit it made a lot more sense after some asshole took my place on PP and I didn't have to walk out there anymore.

I don't remember the exact sequence of events after that first day in the field, but I remember in great detail events that have stayed with me over the years. These events are a constant part of my life; I see them now as if they happened this morning. I will start with the events that I believe happened in the first six months, and then go on to the things that I believe happened in the last six months, or when I was an old-timer.

PART VL

WAR STORIES: FIRST SIX MONTHS

The art of war is simple enough. Find out where your enemy is. Get at him as soon as you can. Strike him as hard as you can, and keep moving on.

<u>Ulysses S. Grant</u>
US general & politician (1822—1885)

DUST-OFF

One day while on a company movement (that's when the whole company moves together, about one hundred men), we were working as a blocking force as part of a battalion operation. I rarely knew what was going on in the big picture, or even in the small picture, except for my squad or platoon's part. I am not sure what was happening, but there was a lot of shooting going on to our front and we were moving toward the shooting as fast as we could. We were going through a pass in the hills and were just coming into a beautiful valley with a stream going through it when something hit a large rock in front of me. I am not sure if it was friendly fire or not, but the rock exploded and hit me with pieces of something and knocked me unconscious. When I came to, medics were all over us. Apparently, five of us were hit and a dust-off had already landed by the beautiful stream. I couldn't hear anything. My ears were ringing, blood was running down my face, and when I looked down I saw the whole front of my body was covered with blood.

I started to run for the dust-off, knowing something wasn't right. The dust-off crew kept waving me on and when I reached the chopper I saw the floor of the ship was covered with other guys flopping around in different states of consciousness. I still couldn't hear anything. I climbed on board and the helicopter took off. Between the roar of the chopper and the ringing in my ears, I was deaf. As the chopper flew, I looked around at the other wounded and the medic/door gunners. Nobody tried to speak to me and I would not have heard if they did. After a little while we came to a hospital. There was a big red cross painted on the chopper pad and medics with white coats and a stretcher came running out to meet our arrival. I could see I was the least wounded in the chopper and hopped out as soon as we landed, to get out of the way of the medics who would be unloading the wounded.

Here is where my problems started. We didn't land at the big U.S. Army hospital at Chu Lai; we landed at some backwater ARVN (Army of the Republic of Vietnam; the South Vietnamese Regular Army) medical station. The people in white coats weren't coming out to unload the chopper; they were bringing out a seriously wounded Arvin (soldier in the ARVN) to be loaded onto the chopper to be transported to Chu Lai. As I jumped out, they were loading their patient into the dust-off, and the chopper took off without me. I stood there with blood dripping down my face, watching the dust-off lift up and disappear into the horizon. As if that wasn't enough, these Arvins came over to me and started talking real fast and pointing at the chopper that left. Even if I could hear them, I would not have understood what they were saying. My Vietnamese at that point was limited to "Stop or I will shoot."

I ignored them because they were gooks and I was tired and my head hurt. I went inside one of the big tents and sat on an empty cot. Some medic-type guy came over and cleaned up my face and what turned out to be several scalp wounds, which bled a lot but were not serious. The blood that I had seen covering my stomach and legs turned out to be purple powder from a smoke grenade that I was wearing on my pistol belt. A one-inch hole in the side of the smoke grenade had been ripped open by shrapnel, and the powder had blown out all over the front of me. It seems that when I first woke up, after being knocked out by the impact, I mistook the purple powder for my own blood and ran in terror toward the dust-off, thinking I was badly wounded. My one bit of luck was that the smoke grenade that had been hanging from my pistol belt had been in front of my balls, which would have been blown off if the smoke grenade had not been there.

I sat there all day with my head wrapped, waiting for another chopper to land so I could jump on it and get back to somewhere that spoke English and where I could figure out what I should do next. I kept going over and over in my head what had happened, and I was afraid of what was going to happen when I got back to the company. It's not like we new guys were treated with any respect at all; we were rarely talked to directly except for an order being barked at us. Our presence was barely noticed except when something dirty or dangerous had to be done, and after it was done there were only complaints about how it wasn't done right, and fucking new green seeds weren't worth shit.

I knew that when I got back to the company this was not going to go well at any level. Not with the captain, not with my lieutenant, and for sure not with my platoon sergeant, who didn't like me anyway. I sat on the cot until the next morning when a resupply chopper came in and I jumped on it. Luckily it landed at LZ Center and I knew where I was. My hearing had pretty much come back except for a slight ringing, and I had a bandage wrapped around my head like a turban. I remember I was thinking about that character in "The Red Badge of Courage," that we had to read in high school. In the book the main character had run off during a battle and ran into a tree. He was afraid to rejoin his company because he thought they knew what he had done and were all talking about him. When he was bandaged up the blood formed a red spot on the bandage, which showed everybody he had been injured, and they accepted him back as a brother-in-arms. I needed a red badge and I didn't have one. I was thinking of cutting open my head with a knife, but I didn't.

When I got off the chopper at LZ Center I went to the aid station, thinking they might justify my injury somehow. They didn't. All they did was take off the bandage, tell me I was all right and to go back to my company. Now I didn't even have a white bandage, showing that at least I had been to a hospital. I went to the chopper pad and told the sergeant there I wanted a chopper out to Black Death. He nodded and told me to stay close, there should be one going out there soon. The chopper finally came and I started my dreaded trip back to the company, trying to think of what I was going to say. I was hoping I would not have been missed, and they would just tell me to go back to my squad. That's not what happened. Apparently if the powers-that-be put an officer in charge of a line company as company commander, those powers actually want him to know where his men are, every day. They have the platoon leaders give a count of their men every night, and the captain calls the number into battalion HQ (headquarters). With me not showing up at the hospital and not being with my squad, all they knew was that I was missing. They didn't know if I had fallen out of the chopper, or wandered off from the chopper pad at Chu Lai, or what had happened.

The yelling started with the company commander, then he called my platoon leader, a second lieutenant up at the CP, to get me the fuck out of there. There was a brief discussion between the two about bringing charges against me for being AWOL (absent without leave) and letting me spend some time in LBJ (Long Binh Jail). This was an in-country prison facility where they sentenced military personnel for misconduct. Any time spent there didn't count toward your 365-day tour of duty. I didn't think they were kidding. My platoon leader put up no defense for me and, in fact, agreed with the commander, saying charges were probably called for in this situation. The captain settled for a "get this piece of shit out of my sight." Of course, no one let me tell my story. They did ask me a few times where

I had been, but when I opened my mouth to answer the yelling got louder. When I got back to my platoon my sergeant started in on me. At that point I stopped listening. All I knew was, I was back to my squad, I wasn't going to jail, and my balls didn't get blown off. All in all, not a bad way to start a day.

OUT OF BODY

About a month or so into my tour, we had been in many firefights. One time our platoon was on patrol and some VC were on high ground and had our platoon pinned down with AK-47 fire. I was still green; when the bullets came in my direction I would lose control and flop around on the ground. I couldn't just quietly lie there, motionless, when bullets were hitting near me. After the firefight, when the gooks had backed off, my platoon sergeant came over to me and took me aside. He told me in a very calm voice that my moving around when we were taking fire was drawing attention to our position. He said if I did it again he was going to shoot me so I would stop. He had that same blank expression, like when he shot that girl. I was more afraid of what he said he was going to do than anything I had experienced so far. I was totally convinced that he would kill me if I moved again in our next firefight. My movements were uncontrollable, a reaction to facing death.

It wasn't long before the firefight started again and I saw he was watching me. If I could have moved or shot back, I would not have been so jittery. But because artillery was being called in, any small arms fire would make it easier for them to see us, so we had to just sit there in a field. As I lay on my back frozen in fear, my mind started to wander and I felt myself floating above my body. I could look down and see myself and the other guys lying there. As I got higher I could see the gooks shooting at us. There weren't many of them and I somehow wasn't afraid anymore. I believe this is what is called an out-of-body experience.

During the rest of my tour of duty I never had another out-of-body experience, but under periods of stress I would go into what I called "slow motion." Everything around me slowed down and normal time would be suspended. I would still be able to move in normal time but people and things around me would slow down to the point where I could see every detail of what was going on. I don't know how else to explain it. It sounds crazy but this "slow motion" saved my life many times.

QUICK DRAW

We were on patrol and came to a small hooch area. I was in the rear of the patrol and didn't see what happened, but our machine gun opened up on the hooch and shot some gooks. I was a rifleman then and went into the hooch with my rifle squad. The squad leader found a blood trail and told me and another grunt, Coats, to follow the trail into the jungle. We followed the trail and didn't get very far before we found a wounded gook crawling on the ground. We called out to our squad leader what we had found and he told us to kill him. The gook was moaning and rolling around on the ground, trying to crawl away. Neither of us could kill him, so the squad leader pushed up through the thick jungle, complaining about what weaklings we were, and put a burst of M-16 rounds into his chest. I remember the squad leader telling two old-timers what had happened, about us not being willing to kill the wounded gook, and them pointing and laughing at us.

We went back to the hooch area and the new lieutenant told me and some other grunts, including Coats, to take up security positions around the perimeter of the hooch area while everybody else got to rest in the cool hooch and look at all the enemy stuff that was left behind. After a while the lieutenant came out of the hooch and yelled at us for not keeping a good lookout. We were looking in at what was going on in the hooch direction and he said we should be looking out, that some gooks could be sneaking in and we wouldn't see them. He went back into the hooch shaking his head in disgust. About five minutes later he came out again and started to walk across the open area in front of the hooch. He was a tall, thin black man and I can still see him as clear as day looking over at me as he walked, drawing his .45-caliber pistol out like a gunslinger in the movies and aiming straight at me. My "slow motion" kicked in and everything slowed down for me; I could see every detail as his finger pulled the trigger.

A gook had crawled up right next to me and had been aiming an SKS rifle at the lieutenant. His single shot took the top of the gook's head off and he lay at my feet on his back with his mouth open. Everybody seemed happy and was congratulating the lieutenant for his good shot and a medic came over to look at the body and went into his medic bag and brought out a pair of pliers. He pulled the gold out of the dead gook's mouth and laughed, showing me and Coats his collection of gold teeth that he kept in a pill bottle. Coats and I looked at each other and slowly shook our heads. Coats started to get a weird look in his eyes.

Later that afternoon, when we were climbing a hill for our night lager (a night defensive perimeter), Coats was in front of me as we walked single file up a very narrow, dangerous path cut into the side of the hill. Coats kept looking back at me, saying something I could not understand. Suddenly, he opened fire with his M-16 and turned toward me, firing all the time. By the time the muzzle was pointed at me he was out of ammo. I called back that Coats had gone nuts and the lieutenant came up and took over. Coats was dusted off when we got to the top of the hill. He rejoined the company a few weeks later and was put in another squad. I would see him from time to time. He started scalping gook women and wearing their scalps as some sort of trophy, tied in a line to a black beret he started wearing. The scalps hung from the beret down his back.

WRONG FOXHOLE

We were night lagered somewhere. I was still kind of new. We had dug our foxholes extra deep that night because word came down that there was movement around the perimeter and we might get hit that night. Another guy and I were at our hole and the next position over was about fifty feet away. The grunt in the foxhole fifty feet away was taking no chances that night and was sleeping in his hole, kind of half in and half out. I was on watch.

It was dark, but I have no idea what time it was when the mortars started coming in. Incoming mortars were particularly dangerous, I had found out, because the trajectory was a high lob and came in almost straight down, so it could come straight into your foxhole. The gooks would set themselves in good positions so that if you returned with small arms fire, they would note your position and zero in with the mortar. The only defense to a mortar attack was to get deep in your foxhole and let the FO (forward observer) call in the artillery. We should then be ready for a ground attack after the mortar fire stopped.

When the mortar fire began, the men on guard duty (each position would have one person on guard duty for one hour, taking turns until sunup) started yelling "Incoming!" and jumping in their foxholes. For some unknown reason the guy at the position fifty feet away got out of his hole, where he was relatively safe, and ran over to our hole and tried to get in. We were already in our hole, me on top and my foxhole buddy under me. The third guy must have gotten confused with all the explosions. A lot of mortar rounds were raining on us, and anybody not in a hole was torn apart by flying shrapnel. He jumped on my back and started pounding me and tearing at my face, screaming at me to let him in. There was no room, so I started punching him back with my fist in his face. He started ripping out my hair and got an arm around my throat and started choking me. I screamed like a wild animal and punched harder with all my strength. I felt his grip grow weaker as the shrapnel started hitting him in the back. He kept screaming in my ear and crying as the mortars came closer to our foxhole. The gooks had zeroed in on us. I could feel the shrapnel hitting his body but he had stopped struggling. After the mortaring stopped I pushed his body off me. I helped some guys wrap his body in his poncho and we carried him up to a chopper pad and put him alongside the other bodies. Nobody ever asked me why he was at our hole or what happened. I guess they all had their stories and they were glad they were alive.

MULE SHOE

One of my first operations was a holding position with another guy called "Mule Shoe" (he was from Mule Shoe, Texas). A holding position was sort of a rear guard. While the main platoon was engaged in a small firefight, Mule Shoe and I were told to guard the back door so the platoon couldn't be attacked from the rear. It was a safe job and we were happy to be assigned it.

I had my machine gun and Mule Shoe had an M-79 grenade launcher. We set up a position in a spot covering the main trail, figuring if anyone came from that direction they would use the trail and we would see them. After about a half-hour, Mule Shoe got restless and said he had to take a shit. There was no good place where he could have some privacy and not get too far from me. He decided to go behind a rock in a small opening to our left. It was in the open but was out of sight of the trail that we were guarding, and he wouldn't be that far from me.

He didn't take his M-79 with him; there was no point. It only held one round and it was not that useful for personal protection. We felt we were in a safe position and didn't have much to worry about. While he was squatting behind the boulder he was shouting out comments about how the Army sucked and you had to shit out in the open like a wild animal. Luckily, I didn't say anything and stayed quiet. Just then a round hit the rock; it had been fired just above my head. A gook was on a short rise about five feet above me. I heard him reload and fire again. It was an SKS bolt action and I could hear him work the bolt to reload. Mule Shoe wasn't hit but he started cussing out the VC.

I could hear the gook turn and start to run. I figured it was a lone sniper, a young kid or woman; he sounded light on his feet. Whoever it was had no idea I was right beneath him. I ran down the side of the rise to ambush him with my pistol. Machine gunners carried a Colt .45 pistol for personal protection. The machine gun was too long and heavy to move around fast, but a .45 could be drawn and fired in the blink of an eye. I was going to wait until I was on top of him, at his back, then cock the .45 and kill him. I was afraid to cock it too soon because we were so close he would have heard the sound of the metal slide on the pistol and I would have lost my advantage. I preferred to take a chance and wait until he was in sight, then it would be too late for him to react. On the other hand, if he somehow knew I was coming and had his weapon cocked and ready to shoot, I would not have enough time to cock the pistol and shoot, even though it would only take a fraction of a second to get a round off. There was nobody else, just him and me, and I realized right then and there I was really going to kill another human being.

The only reason I didn't kill him was that he ran left at the bottom of the rise. If he had run to the right, he would have come out just in front of me and I would have cocked the pistol and shot him in the back, or in the chest if he turned around. I would not have missed, I would not have hesitated, my hand would not have trembled, and I would not have put the pistol down and let him go. If I wounded him, I would keep on shooting until he was dead. If the pistol failed to kill him for any reason, I would have killed him with my bare hands. Had he turned right instead of left, he would have been dead. At that moment I realized I was a killer. Not necessarily a murderer, but a killer for sure. Even though I had not killed that person, I knew in my heart I was ready to.

ON-THE-JOB TRAINING

I was starting to get the hang of how things worked (OJT). I had graduated from rifleman to grenadier (carrying an M-79 grenade launcher) to my final position of machine gunner. I had not done well in basic training in the physical part because of all those tests—monkey bars, obstacle courses, and climbing ropes. They were designed to test your general agility and athletic abilities. All that didn't mean shit now. We were draft animals. I was a large guy, 225 pounds, so it was easier for me to carry a 75-pound load than a guy weighing 125 pounds. The lieutenant gave me the machine gun because the machine gunner carried the largest load.

One day we were lagered on a flat sight in deep jungle. I had begun to understand some basic tactics of what we were doing and I knew lagering on a flat sight, with no open fields of fire, was not good. What was worse was that we were staying there that night. Nighttime was "Charlie Time." Air support didn't fly at night. The idea was to hunt the gooks during the day, through search and destroy missions, and find a good defensible hiding position at night. That was Charlie's time to get some payback. Without helicopter gun ships, jet fighters, bombers, fixed-winged observation planes, and anything else we could use to support us during the day, we were not as effective as ground troops. The fight became much fairer. We lost our edge at night and the gooks moved freely, going anywhere they wanted. It was not wise in 1968 for an infantry company in our AO (area of operation) to be on flat ground without clear fields of fire when the sun went down.

The problem was, we were constantly getting a new commanding officer. He had to go through his OJT but we had to pay the price. On this night my machine gun squad was sent with some riflemen to pull an ambush on the main trail. They also sent three Arvins with us, which was a first. Our standard operational procedure for an ambush was to go out to a main path just after dark, follow it up about a quarter mile, and find a good place to set up the machine gun. Once the machine gun was set up in place with a nice open field of fire, the rifleman would find places to support the gun, it being the heaviest weapon, and the weapon that would kill the most enemy coming down the path. If that happened we would shoot everything we had, radio the company CP that we had sprung the ambush and we were coming in, then grab what we could and run as fast as we could back to the company before the gooks could regroup and come after us.

After a while I had refined the ambush with a few additions. In AIT we were taught the only defense to a good ambush was to run directly at the ambush firing line, screaming and firing. This would be the last thing they would expect. If, when the trap was sprung, you got down on the ground or started to run, you would be easily killed. They would have fire superiority, that is, the momentum, and they could just stand up and keep shooting until you were all dead, even if the group being ambushed outnumbered the ambushers ten-to-one. This I truly understood. Being on ambush every third night, I got plenty of practice. Now that I was in charge of the ambush we could do it my way.

What I would do when I picked the ambush site was this: I would stand where the gooks would be when I sprang the ambush, and look around to see where I would hide if I was them and someone started to shoot at me. It wasn't hard to find out where they would jump for cover—a ditch, tree, or thick brush.

Then we would set up a claymore mine that could be remotely fired from our position when the survivors of the initial opening fire jumped for cover. After a while I found the claymore bulky and hard to hide if there was moonlight, so I experimented with detonating cord and C-4 plastic explosive, always setting up the secondary blasts myself. I became aware that a lot of the guys I came to the company with were not there anymore, and I didn't trust the new guys with anything this important.

On this night we started to set up our usual ambush. The three Arvins came up to me and said they were going out to catch a live prisoner and they wanted me to go with them. These guys must have been the Special Forces of the South Vietnamese Army. Usually, Arvins were happy to let us do the fighting and they would only come along for the ride. These guys weren't like that. They were going down the path to a hooch area they seemed to know about to see if any VC were there. They told me to take off my equipment, helmet, and anything else that was hard and would make noise. They only wanted me to take the .45 pistol that I always carried.

Off we went down the trail on our little adventure. I didn't have to go; I couldn't care less about winning the war or killing gooks. I saw them as just another group of dumb fucks that didn't get out of the draft either. I think I went because I didn't have to go. This was my decision and I could do it without asking anybody else and that made me feel good. Besides, it was anybody's guess what was more dangerous: staying there at the ambush with the other guys or going off on a lark with these Arvins. If the company got hit really hard that night, the first thing the enemy would try to do would be to kill all the OPs (observation posts) and ambushers. If we were off on our little trip we could keep low and come back in after the fighting was over. Something was going to happen that night—I could feel it.

We got to the first hooch area and nobody was there except a couple of old mama sans (pigeon for older Vietnamese women) chewing beetle nut and gibbering back and forth. We moved quietly up on the hooch and made sure who was inside before the Arvins went inside. They told me to wait outside and stand guard because their mama sans didn't like GIs and if they knew I was there they wouldn't talk. I wasn't surprised; nobody liked us. They came back after some gook talk and some yelling and we started off again down another trail. I had no idea where I was and if I got separated from these guys for any reason I would be hopelessly lost, with no equipment, and would not know my way back to the ambush or the company. I stayed close.

We came to another hooch area and the same thing happened again. On the third try we crept up slowly. Something was happening inside and it wasn't old female gooks talking. As we got closer we could see inside because there was a candle burning. A young man dressed in black pajamas, traditional Viet Cong clothing, was on top of a young woman, fucking her with his AK-47 leaning up against the wall. We all smiled at seeing this and we rushed into the hooch, grabbing the VC and his weapon. After some laughter from the Arvins, we took the VC outside and tied his hands. They asked for my pistol. The head Arvin cocked the .45 and put it in the VC's mouth and said something in Vietnamese to another guy. The other guy held the .45 in the VC's mouth and the head guy went into the hooch and repeatedly raped the young Vietnamese girl. After he was done, the other two took turns raping her while I held my .45 in the VC's mouth. When they were done, they offered me a turn with the young girl, not wanting to be rude to their guest, and I declined. They gagged the VC and we started back down the path toward where the rest of our men at the ambush were waiting for us. We hadn't gone very far when I heard a burst of M-16 fire coming from the hooch area. As I looked back I saw one of the Arvins running toward us; he had killed the young girl.

When we got back to the ambush we were told that the radio was buzzing with activity because of enemy movement around the company perimeter. Apparently the gooks were probing the main position, looking for weak spots, and the company was on full alert. We requested to bring our prisoner back through the company lines. Our request was denied. They told us to get far away from the company's location. They were going to start calling in artillery at prearranged locations, and the company couldn't risk letting us back in. They said we should hide in the jungle and come back in the morning when the gunships could see what they were doing. I didn't want to do this. I felt ashamed of what I had taken part in and wanted to get away from these Arvin murderers. I especially wanted to get away from the VC we had caught; he kept looking at me. He must have sensed I was ashamed of what happened and kept looking at me with disgust. We did what we were told and slunk off into the jungle, listening to the artillery exploding around the company position. Flares were shot up all night, lighting up the area, until finally the sun came up and they figured it was safe to let us come in.

When we got back to the company, there was a lot of activity going on. A chopper pad was set up and supplies and personnel were coming in on choppers. We had no position on the company perimeter to go to because we were out all night, so we found a place to lie down out of the way. The Arvins brought the prisoner over to the CP and there seemed to be a lot of laughing and backslapping going on. Another chopper came in, this one with some big shot ARVN brass on board. They got off and went over to the CP and all the laughing and backslapping started again. The commotion was about the prisoner. The three Arvins that I was with the night before started to interrogate the prisoner in front of their brass. After they beat him with their rifle butts and kicked him until they were tired, the head guy took out some pliers and started to work on his toes. I could see the prisoner had shit and pissed himself, which seemed to bring great laughter from the ARVN brass, and our officers went along with the fun. I didn't know a lot of Vietnamese but I could tell this guy told them everything he knew and probably made up some stuff he thought they wanted to hear.

After they were done with him the head Arvin tried to get the prisoner up off the ground, trying to get him to run for freedom toward the jungle. The guy was a bloody mess but he somehow got up and started to run. The head Arvin extended one arm with his M-16 in his hand and slowly fired one round at a time into the back of the prisoner, walking toward him as the guy fell, emptying his eighteen rounds into the guy we caught fucking the night before. I noticed a new face in the group of laughing personnel. This was our new platoon leader, Lieutenant Somebody. I thought it odd, that this new lieutenant who had been in the field all of forty-five minutes—he came in on the last chopper—was laughing at what I was sure was the first person he saw being tortured and murdered. A few months later on Thanksgiving Day, when some other guys and I were holding him, trying to stop a sucking chest wound that he got in an ambush we walked into, I wondered as I watched him dying, his face losing color, if he thought this was funny. I had never forgiven him for giving in to peer pressure and laughing at that VC. I plan on bringing it up the next time I see him.

This might be a good time to mention that the Arvins were on our side, the good guys. They were afraid to be captured by the VC because they knew what every grunt knew, or should have known. The VC didn't take prisoners and hold you in a prisoner of war camp like in World War II. Sure, you saw a lot of POWs (prisoners of war) being released after the war was over, but those guys were mostly military personnel shot down over North Vietnam. What happened to this guy was what was in store for any one of us who was unlucky enough or stupid enough to be captured alive.

WAR STORIES: LAST SIX MONTHS

AMBUSH—I

The company lagered at a refugee camp in a place called Happy Valley. Lagering there was considered a real bit of luck for all of us. We'd been running patrols out of there for a couple of days when the orders came down to run a joint mission with the PFs (Popular Forces, South Vietnamese National Guard–type local military units) the following morning. We showed up at their village the next morning with our entire rifle company, about one hundred men. The PFs had another one hundred men and they were told to mix in with our men in a single file formation. Running a patrol with anything over twenty men in that area didn't make sense. The land was too flat and we would be seen a mile away. I noticed that only about half of the PFs had weapons—odd. This whole operation started to have a bad smell. It was hard to believe our colonel would send us on such a sloppy mission, until I realized this was political. I didn't know what was going on, but I did know when military missions started to be run by politics, the grunts got hurt.

We humped a long way into what the PF guys called Viet Cong Valley. Once in the valley we passed a few hooch areas and went directly to a large village. The village was mostly empty and we set up a lager site and rested. The GIs rested while the PFs went to work. They started taking everything that wasn't nailed down. They took rice baskets and loaded them up with live chickens, ducks, a goat or two, clothes, and stuff I didn't even recognize. Half their guys didn't carry weapons; they were there to plunder the village and were using us as their muscle. This was armed robbery and we didn't like being used like that. We started back, with or without the PFs, and what had been a clumsy troop movement coming turned into an almost comical procession marching back. We must have looked like a caravan without the camels, just loads of stuff packed high on our backs.

It started to rain real hard and that was when the VC started to snipe at us. I related our situation to the Revolutionary War in New England. We marched down the trails like the redcoats, stretched out for a mile, and the VC attacked our flanks at will, like the minutemen did to the English. I didn't like it. It took about five hours to march back, with firefights breaking out all along the trail. Every time a firefight broke out, the machine gun would be called for so my men and I would have to run down the trail tripping over the PFs hauling their loot. We ran out of ammo a few times. Both times we had to call in slicks to bring ammo, and I could see they barely made it in the heavy rain. I don't think we killed one gook all day but they got their share of hits in. They dogged us all the way back to the refugee camp. We had taken their stuff and they wanted it back. The next day nobody went out on patrol; we stayed home and licked our wounds.

Our new lieutenant decided that our platoon could go out at night and set up an ambush to catch these VC in the morning, when they seemed to be coming. We kept getting new lieutenants, and each time they came in raring to go, trying to make a name for themselves and impress the battalion hierarchy, and we just kept getting more tired. This one seemed to be doing all right. He set us up to be going out at midnight. We set up on the flatlands in some bushes in a classic L-shaped ambush and waited. I fell asleep and when I woke up I could see this Gary, an old-timer, aiming his M-16 through the bushes like he was going to shoot. I had conked out completely and missed out on seeing the VC come sneaking out slowly. I was later told they moved very slowly in the open, always looking for cover. By the time I had awakened, the VC had been moving slowly right into the killing zone of our ambush. What I saw when I awoke was Gary springing the trap by killing the closest VC. I couldn't see anything and everybody started firing, so I stood up, holding the M-60 by my side, and cut down most of the gooks, who were surprisingly close. The ones out of range ran off.

We had this Chieu Hoi (an ex–Viet Cong who changed sides) with us named Wong who was now making a very good living working for the U.S. government as a bounty hunter. He worked out of this refugee camp we were lagered near and decided there might be some good money to be made tagging along with us that night. Wong worked by the piece, so much for a captured AK-47, so much for an SKS rifle, and so much for a set of VC ears. He quickly ran out to collect the weapons off the dead gooks, which didn't take long, but harvesting the ears seemed to be time consuming.

As the rest of our platoon stood around waiting for Wong to cut off their ears (he was busting out their gold teeth, too), I noticed the VC were regrouping. They must have stopped running and realized there weren't very many of us compared to them, and started to come back in our direction. They were still out of range but I fired my gun in the VC's direction, getting the attention of the platoon sergeant and the lieutenant. I motioned to them that the gooks were coming back and we'd better get going. They both realized I was right and we left. That's the first time I seemed to get any appreciation from my superiors. The lieutenant told me later he thought I did a good job by noticing the gooks coming back, which could have proven embarrassing, us just standing and the gooks coming back and killing us. Of course, he didn't know I had fallen sound asleep during the night when we all should have been on highest alert.

AMBUSH—2

After that ambush we felt pretty good about ourselves. The new lieutenant, trying to impress the captain I am sure, offered our services for another ambush. This time we were to go the other way, across a small river and into a very thick jungle. The plan was to go out on a day patrol and scout out a hooch area that was in the intersection of three main trails. We were going to stop at the hooch, looking like we were taking a rest, make some excuse to get mad at the local gooks, and shoot their dogs. Hooch areas like this always had dogs. The dogs acted partly as alarms to warn the villagers of strangers approaching, and partly as a food source. An alarm system you could eat. We had to kill the dogs so they wouldn't bark when we came back that night to set up our ambush.

The lieutenant assigned us each to exact places where he wanted us to be when we went back that night. He had us practice our positions in an open, dry rice paddy so everybody knew exactly where they should be and where everybody else should be, so we wouldn't shoot each other. It's called knowing your fields of fire—a very important concept in thick jungle ambushes like this, where you couldn't see more than a few feet in front of you in broad daylight, never mind at night. This lieutenant performed his job well and made sure we were prepared, and that was good. But if he hadn't been trying so hard to impress the captain, we wouldn't be doing these risky operations that needed careful preparation, and that was bad.

We rested, and got up around midnight to set up the ambush. He had us paint our faces with camo stick, more careful preparations than we ever needed before, and we headed out. It went smooth as silk. We slipped into the village without a sound. Nobody said a word and everybody knew exactly where to go because of the practice sessions. We set up an L-shaped ambush on a curve in the main trail. Three riflemen were set in the bush, well hidden, on the side of the trail. Just past them, I was set up with my machine gun in the middle of the trail just past the curve, so I couldn't be seen by anybody walking down the trail. Our position wasn't perfect; the cover in front of me on the curve was thin and you could see through it, but the movements went smoothly and now it was time to wait for our prey.

The night passed and nothing happened. I wasn't about to fall asleep this time. I had been lucky on the other ambush a few days before and I wasn't going to repeat that mistake. Daybreak came and with the light we decided to have a well-deserved cigarette. Our spirits were up because nothing had happened and we were probably going back to the camp soon for some food and rest. We couldn't talk or make any sound but my assistant gunner Peter and I communicated through facial expressions. We spent every waking moment together and could read each other's thoughts. Peter reached over to give me a light and as I went to grab it, I saw three people come around the corner.

My slow motion wasn't working and everything happened in a blur. I can still see the three people standing there frozen when they saw me—two small children in front and a young mother with her arms around them, as she walked into them when they stopped abruptly at seeing me. Just then shots fired out as the NVA, who had been using the mother and her children as a point unit, reached the riflemen hiding alongside the trail. The riflemen had seen the young mother and her children coming and had let them pass, but when the NVA got alongside of them, about three feet away, they opened up and shot as many as they could. I saw the three just as the firing started and stood up, shouting for everybody to get down, and started firing in the direction of the small family and the NVA.

The mother and kids dropped first, then the uniformed solders started to go down as I methodically raked the area, making sure I lowered my fire after the initial burst. I was trained to compensate for everybody dropping to the ground, their instinctive action after their first shock. It was fight or flight, and I didn't want these guys going into a flight mode and turning and rushing us. They could have saved themselves if instead of running for their lives they had rushed us. I would have killed a lot fewer of them and they would have overrun us in a minute. But human instincts are what they are, no matter if your eyes are round or slanted, so they ran and died.

When I had gone through about 250 rounds, and Peter had reloaded twice, I stopped firing and stood there, kind of saying, "Oh shit, look what I did." I heard a child's voice crying out in pain. A short blast of an M-16 stopped the noise and I turned around, starting back to a prearranged rallying point. We met the lieutenant and the other members of the platoon and I said one word to the lieutenant, "NVA," nothing more. Nothing more had to be said. We had ambushed an NVA troop movement and we headed down the main trail toward the river about a mile away, where our company was to meet us if something like this happened.

The river separated the thick jungle from the open rice paddies and it was there we would pull back to, letting the artillery do the rest of the work. We didn't get very far down the path when the lieutenant realized there were some men missing. I found out later they had fallen asleep and woke with all the shooting going on and got confused and took the wrong trail to the rallying point. The lieutenant sent back two men to find them, and we stooped down as low as we could get and waited for them to get back. We squatted there on the main trail in total silence, waiting for our men to rejoin us. The waiting hurt. It was like a vise was on my head, squeezing me more and more as the seconds dragged by. My shock at what had just happened was starting to wear off and my body screamed for action. I was in total flight mode and felt physical pain from not being able to run down the trail.

Just then we all heard a low rumble. I swear it sounded like a stampede of cattle, and it was getting louder. I could see what had happened in my mind's eye. When we sprang the ambush just minutes before, we must have really spooked these guys. They were NVA troops, which meant they weren't from around here and were just passing through, probably using local VC as guides. We must have killed the locals in the ambush, and the NVA ran off amok, aimlessly running through the jungle, out of control. At first I thought they might be trying to cut us off from our escape, but we had hit them too fast. They would have no way of telling where we were, never mind where we were going, and no time to put together a plan and carry it out. No, these troops were running flat out through the jungle, not in single file but abreast, as a mob. I guess they weren't trained as well as I had heard, or maybe they were all replacements and had never been in enemy contact before. Either way, they were running straight toward us. I don't think they even knew a main trail was there. I was positive as they came closer they had no idea we were squatting there, waiting for our tardy comrades. As the thundering herd of NVA troops came closer, I could hear the individual yelps of pain from people crying out as they tore themselves through the thick jungle.

I was next to the lieutenant and I saw his M-16 rise up to take aim. They were close but not right at us yet. I grabbed the barrel of his rifle and pulled it down. I made a hand signal for him to wait and he did, looking at me questioningly. When the gooks were ten feet from us, I yelled, "Now!" and let his barrel go and stood up firing like I had done less than ten minutes before in the initial ambush. Just then the lost men rejoined us and started firing, too. The result was total chaos in the NVA mob. I saw total surprise in their faces as we popped up in front of them. Their faces twisted in terror as we cut them down from such a close distance. I don't think they even attempted to return fire. The fight part of their "fight or flight" primal behavior was tucked far away in their brains. These guys were in full flight mode.

We turned on them like you see in the old Westerns, when the cowboys turn the lead steers in a stampede and the rest of the herd follows. When we all ran out of ammo and the rest of the herd was still coming—I had no idea there were so many of them—our own "flight" mode kicked in and everybody, including the lieutenant, started to run down the trail toward the safety of the open rice paddy and the rest of our company, who were surely at the river waiting for us. We elbowed each other for a position as we raced down the path for safety. My twenty-three–pound machine gun slowed me down some, but with it riding on my shoulder I was able to knock others on the head if they tried to pass me, without taking it from my shoulder or losing my stride. Part of the "flight" process is the fear of being left behind.

I am sure the NVA were not running after us, but I didn't want anybody to pass me, putting fewer people between the gooks and me. When we got to the river, I jumped from the bank and I swear I landed halfway across. The river was only two feet deep and as I landed the gun fell from me and landed in the water. I left the gun there and got it later, after the artillery bombarded the entire area where the NVA had been. When we got back to the camp, I started to drink a warm beer that I had in my pack and some of my comrades came up to me and said it wasn't my fault that I killed the kids and their mother. For some reason I never felt ashamed of killing that family. I had no choice; I felt my duty was to me first and my fellow comrades second.

Later I heard guys talking about me having balls of steel. Apparently the lieutenant had been telling the story of me holding him back from firing on the trail, so the NVA could get closer and we could kill more. People see what they want to see. I was holding him back from firing because I was hoping the NVA wouldn't see us and might pass us by without us ever having to fire a shot. It's just when they got so close that I panicked and jumped, shouting to fire. I laughed at how he had misinterpreted my actions, and I was almost insulted that he would think I would risk my life and others just to kill more gooks.

This guy was a lifer and was trying to build a career, and from his point of view that would be the only reason I would hold back from shooting sooner. I was just a draftee grunt using every bit of energy I had to get home. On the other hand, it didn't hurt having a reputation as having balls of steel, living with a group of men constantly infighting over food, water, and who got the last poundcake out of the last case of C-rations. I never disputed the story and let the rep stand.

The character of every act depends upon the circumstances in which it is done.
<u>Oliver Wendell Holmes Jr.</u>
US jurist (1841—1935)

AMBUSH—3

On one company movement, I don't remember where, there were no trails so we had to walk up a stream that meandered through a never-ending landscape of low hills. We had humped all day and didn't stop until after sundown, just before dark. It was my gun squad's turn to go out on ambush and we went out with a rifle squad run by a guy named Clint. I liked Clint and thought him a competent squad leader, meaning he wouldn't do anything stupid and get us killed. Clint and I had come to the company at the same time and although we were always in different squads, I thought of him as a very decent person, someone who was dealt a hand and would do the best he could without losing too much self-dignity.

We moved about a hundred yards downstream in the direction we had just come from, looking for a good ambush site. We found a perfect site—a small knoll rising about ten feet overlooking the stream bed. It was the only approach to the company's location and it had nice clean white sand to lie in; we were all very tired. Best of all, the site backed up to an almost vertical rock wall. This would protect our back and we would only have to worry about the enemy coming at us from one direction.

We set up the machine gun in the middle, with riflemen along both my sides, and lay down in prone positions with everybody having a good view of the direction the enemy would have to come. We would all take turns, one at a time, watching the streambed for movement, all night long. The reason it was nice that everybody had a good view from where they lay was that there would be less movement as the guard changed every hour all night long. All the new guy on guard duty had to do was take the PRC-25 (the radio) from the last guy, and keep one ear on the phone handset listening for messages from the company CP, and the other ear open for sounds from the stream bed. Not having to move each time a new guy took his turn meant we could be quieter. Being quiet on an ambush was a good thing.

I woke up wide-awake. Something was wrong and I hadn't figured out what it was yet. I looked down at the stream and saw and heard nothing. The stream bed was all right but something was definitely wrong. Everybody else was awake and bug-eyed. No one said anything because talking would make a sound and on an ambush you didn't want to make a sound. I realized what it was everybody was listening to, but I couldn't believe it. We heard movement above us. What we thought was a perfect ambush site turned out to be located just beneath where some gooks decided to climb down the side of a very steep hill and set themselves up in a position for I couldn't guess what.

They were making quite a bit of noise as they climbed down the side of the hill. They stopped climbing about fifteen feet right above us. We started to hear digging noises and I still couldn't figure out what they were doing. They had no clue we were there and we lay frozen in our movements. There was no way we could turn around and shoot them without them cutting us down. If we were on flat ground we could easily have lobbed a few grenades on their position and then, after the shock of the blast, moved in and shot the ones who didn't die in the grenade blast. These guys were fifteen feet above us. If any grenades were thrown they would roll back down on us. If we made any sound at all and they realized we were there, all they had to do was toss grenades down on us or pick us off as we scrambled beneath them.

I felt we were in no position to do anything. We should just let them bury whatever it was they were burying, and go away the same way they had come. We could return to the company the next morning, keeping our mouths shut about the gooks. It would be too hard to explain why we didn't do anything, and nobody would ever know what happened. I had decided a while back if I was going to make it out of Vietnam alive and somehow make it back to Connecticut, eight thousand miles away, I was going to have to take some control of my own destiny. I was going to have to list my options, and take action.

When the first mortar went off, no one was more surprised than me. We could not talk while the digging was going on because they were so close, and it had never occurred to me they were setting up a mortar tube. When I heard the first thump of the mortar coming out of the tube, I realized immediately what was going on. I also realized immediately what our situation was as far as contacting the company. I looked at Clint, and without a word exchanged we agreed not to tell the company that we knew where the mortar was. We had become partners in crime. The crime was this: as soon as the first mortar round exploded within the company perimeter, the CP would be on the radio calling all the LPs (listening posts) and the two main ambushes, asking if they could see the flash of the mortar tube. If they could see the flash they would be expected to direct artillery fire on the location of the flash, stopping the mortars.

Each rifle company had an FO (forward observer), an officer with an artillery battery on a fire support base. The thought was that if one of their own officers was in the field in direct radio contact with his battery, their aim might be a little better, and they all spoke the same artillery jargon so the communication would be better. The FOs changed all the time, so the officer at the battery directing the firing tonight might be the FO in the field the next night. A lot of good infantrymen lost their lives through misdirected artillery fire (friendly fire). Because the area was so hilly, the FO had no idea where the mortars were coming from. The only defense for a mortar attack on an infantry company was to locate the mortar and take it out with artillery. If that didn't work, dig in and wait until the gooks ran out of rounds. When the CP contacted you on the radio, they didn't expect you to say anything. They would ask you a question and have you respond by breaking squelch. They would say something like, "Can you see the mortar flash? Break squelch once for 'yes' and twice for 'no'."

When the first round exploded in the company lager site, the company CPs went crazy on the radio. They started asking all the platoons if anyone could see the mortar flash. The platoons' CPs could talk and nobody knew where the flash was coming from. The company CP asked us if we knew where the mortar was. I had taken over the radio from the man on duty. This was it—if I broke squelch once they would be all over us, asking where it was and if we could correct the artillery fire. They would never let us stay put. We would have to show our presence to the gooks right over our heads by moving or directing the artillery fire on ourselves. It was bad enough that there was a full moon that night, exposing our dark bodies lying on the soft white sand to the gook's position, but each time a mortar went off the light from the flash exposed us even more. It also let us see each other's faces, which I didn't want either.

I broke squelch twice, telling them "no," we did not know where the mortar was. They asked a few more times, saying it seemed to be coming from our direction, but I knew sound in these hills bounced all around and the company CP would never know for sure it came from fifteen feet above our heads. The rounds finally stopped, and we heard the gooks laughing as they collected all their stuff and walked off, safe and sound. As we walked toward the company the next morning Clint and

I stopped everybody to get our story straight in case anybody asked. Isn't that what criminals do? The other men agreed on silence, knowing full well what we had done. Clint had one green seed who was puzzled as to what had happened and didn't understand why he should keep quiet. I reached out and slowly pulled him toward me. I said very calmly that if he said anything at all to anyone, I would find out and kill him. My face was expressionless. Clint nodded his head in agreement. After that night Clint and I avoided each other.

This was our Company Patch "The Grim Reaper"
We placed these patches on the bodies of he V.C. we killed so
the other V.C. would know who killed them

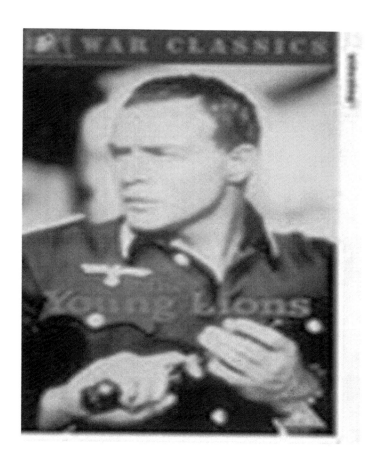

The Young Lions (<u>1958</u>)
This is the movie I had seen as a kid.

THE ISLAND

At this point I was no longer a new guy. I wasn't an old-timer yet, but I was my own guy. When we first got to the company, all us new guys hung together like sheep, but now we were spreading out and taking charge of things, in small ways.

Before that lieutenant died, he brought us out on a patrol in the flatlands, with orders to check out a village on an island. The island wasn't on a body of water like an ocean or a lake, but was in the middle of a huge rice paddy. Rice paddies are impossible to walk through unless you walk on dikes, which have small paths about two feet wide, wide enough that only one man can walk at a time and a group can only walk single file. This made for a unique situation for us to approach the village, and a great defense barrier for the village. If they were approached by U.S. troops and they opened fire, the troops could only jump into the rice paddies.

It is hard to describe how bad the rice paddies smelled. One thousand years of water buffalo shit and human shit go into these paddies, not to mention the snakes, spiders, and other nasty critters that live in these cesspools. There were two feet of mud that a man cannot run through, and if you tried, you would soon get bogged down and be an easy target from the village. There were only two ways into the island village: There was a dike on each side, and they were heavily guarded night and day, we were told.

The rice field was about to be harvested and the VC took control of the village to confiscate all of the rice. It was suggested we just call in artillery and wipe the village off the map, but then who would harvest the rice that was needed for the locals to live on? Why these locals didn't just pack their bags and leave, instead of trying to live in a battle zone, was beyond me. Of course, where would they go? The whole country was a battle zone. Anyway, our platoon was given the job to check out the village and see what the situation was.

By this time, platoon sergeant "Lip" was gone and I was enjoying a much higher position in the pecking order of our platoon. I was squad leader of the platoon machine gun squad. This meant I was in charge of both machine guns in the platoon, so I got to position the guns, our heaviest firepower, at night lager and during day operations. I was actually getting some respect from my platoon leader and the new platoon sergeant. I still had not forgiven the lieutenant for laughing at the VC prisoner, but things were getting better for me in platoon life. All this would change.

The land around the rice paddy was very flat. We were trying to get to the village before the sun came up, so the choppers bringing us out used their standard operational procedure when inserting small units of troops into an area. They would land in one location, then lift up and go a few miles and land again, and keep on doing this three or four times. The idea was not to let Charlie know where the unit was getting off, because they were always watching out for choppers bringing in units. Once they knew where you were they would stalk you, waiting for an opportunity to sweep in and wipe out the unit before it could radio for help and get in either gunships for support or slicks (Hueys) for an extraction.

This exercise wasn't needed in the mountainous area where we usually operated, because the mountains and valleys made it hard for anyone to see very far and the valley played tricks with the loud sound of choppers. Sometimes if a chopper was in the next valley you couldn't even hear it. Where we were going, you could hear and see a chopper coming from ten miles away or more.

So we were on the choppers doing these waltzes and we all got off on the second landing, letting the choppers take off and play their charade. We walked in the dark for about an hour. The walking was very easy, on flat land with wide, well-used trails, which meant no booby traps. We got to the edge of the rice paddy with the village in it and set up in a holding position to figure out what to do next. The lieutenant and the platoon sergeant were talking about how to approach the village without being caught out in the paddies and cut apart. We had about twenty men in the platoon and no backup. Because we were so far from our company, and out of range of the fire support base's artillery, if something happened it would take a while to get help. On the other hand, we could just as easily walk across the paddy, enter the village with no VC there, just locals getting ready to go out and work the fields, and sit down and have a smoke while enjoying the beautiful view. Then we could hang around until the chopper came and picked us up, landing on the island because it was safe now.

Here is where I got involved. They actually asked me what my opinion was. They came over to me and my gun crew and went out of their way, in front of my crew, to ask what I thought we should do—go in while it was still dark or wait a little while until it got light. Both ways had their obvious pros and cons. I listened to both sides, and they waited for my reply as I stood there, seeming to ponder the dilemma.

What I was thinking about was a movie I had seen, "The Young Lions," starring Dean Martin and Marlon Brando. Brando played a young German officer in the Africa Corps during World War II who was in the same position I was. In Hollywood style, he looked back over his shoulder and pointed out to his superior that the sun would be up in a few minutes. The bright morning sun would be at their backs and directly in the eyes of the enemy, who were just waking up for the day. He told them if they waited a few minutes they could take the whole camp and not lose any men. They waited, it worked great, and he looked good to his superiors.

This all flashed through my mind in seconds. My hesitation was, did I have the courage to present this plan for all to see? Would they laugh at me, was the sun really in the right position to be in the eyes of the people in the village, friend or foe, and most of all, had anyone else seen that movie? Not easy questions, but I looked over my shoulder and saw the first break of light. The sun would be in the perfect position, so I said the words. They were impressed, agreed, and we waited for the sun to come up. The sun came up that morning and, being in the flatlands, there were no shadows. It was as bright as could be; looking at it would burn your retinas.

We walked into the village totally unopposed. Once in the village, not on the edge or at the outside hooches, but right in the middle of the village, the Viet Cong and us realized at the same time we were in the middle of their camp. There was an explosion of shooting and grenades going off. My plan worked perfectly, only to lead us right into this meat grinder. We had caught them totally by surprise, but there were about a hundred of them. I don't remember much of what happened next. Everyone was running around shooting every which way. A lot of people got shot in the first couple of minutes; we were only a few feet from them. Somehow our platoon regrouped in one part of the village. Gunships had been called in and we popped smoke to let the air support know where we were.

Most of the Viet Cong ran out of the village on the other side, using the narrow path on the dike for their escape. The gun ships showed up really fast, and had a field day with the VC who hadn't made it to the jungle yet and were running in the open. The few VC who stayed and fought after the initial surprise were torn apart by the gunships. When I wrote this down it seemed like this was a real successful mission, and maybe it was as far as body count goes, but we all knew we almost died or, worse, became prisoners of the Viet Cong. We knew what happened to prisoners.

See, if we had waited until full light, the VC would have only shot our point men, the green seeds, and we probably could have fallen back and called for help. These weren't your garden variety VC, farmers during the day and out running around at night in black pajamas, setting up booby traps or sniping at the Americans when they could. These were hard-core Viet Cong, fully supplied with web gear, RPGs (rocket-propelled grenades), mortars, and a lot of mortar rounds. These guys weren't passing through like most of the regular Viet Cong or NVA (North Vietnamese Army), on their way to attack some big city on the coast. These troops were probably sent there to get the rice. My fancy Hollywood trick had only gotten us into the belly of the beast, and if things had not gone just right, or there had been more of them, they would have killed us all in their own special way. The lieutenant never asked for my opinion again, and that was all right with me.

I heard later that villagers from a refugee camp harvested the rice. Another infantry company went out with them each day, packing all the workers onto a Chinook. The infantry came in on Hueys and stayed all day, and everybody went back to camp at night until the rice was all picked.

"A Jewish friend and I used to argue about who carried more guilt, Irish Catholics or Jews. After he read my book, he told me I won."

Robert B Boyd Jr.

OPERATION RICE BOWL

We went on a major operation called "Operation Rice Bowl." There was a good size river on the edge of our AO we called the Big Blue. We didn't cross it very often because there were no bridges across it. There wasn't much there except jungle and mountains—not hills but mountains, the kind it would take an infantry company two or three days to climb. They weren't the kind of mountains you used ropes to climb, but the kind that had thick jungle all the way up to the top. On the other side of this vast area was the Laotian border and the Ho Chi Minh Trail.

The gooks had a free hand in this area. They took a left off the Ho Chi Minh Trail and headed toward the Big Blue on their way to Da Nang or any of the other big east coast cities. The brass must have gotten fed up with their free rein in the area and decided to launch Operation Rice Bowl. Somebody picked out a mountain in the middle of this God-awful uninhabited jungle and said this is where we'll set up a new temporary fire support base.

A Special Forces unit went in first, before dawn, and secured the top of the hill. Our rifle company got CAed (combat assaulted) at the break of dawn and set up a perimeter around the hilltop. I was on the first wave of slicks and got pushed out of the chopper and landed on my back. I lay on my back like a turtle, my hands and feet waving around in the air until I could roll to one side and get up. I hated getting pushed out of choppers. The LZ didn't seem to be hot, but as we came in on the slicks we could see there were only four or five Special Forces guys and they had secured only a small flat part on the top of the hill, big enough to land four slicks at once. The rest of the hill was unsecured and needed searching.

Another rifle company came in after us. The hill was secure by then and the choppers actually landed and let the troops get out on their own. About thirty minutes after the hill was declared secure, a Chinook brought in a bulldozer and it started digging a hole on top of the hill. When the hole was finished, a Chinook brought in a big metal box about forty feet long and dropped it in the hole. We were told this would be the command post and the colonel would be there for the next three days—RHIP (rank has its privileges). It must be nice to travel with your personal portable steel bunker.

We were actually on a ridge line, not just a round hilltop, so both ends of the ridge had to have an OP and be manned with a squad of infantry at all times. Our company was at one end of the ridge and our platoon had to take turns with the other three platoons in manning the OP. When it was my squad's turn to go out and relieve the OP, I rebelled for the first time. The lieutenant came down to my position and told me to get my squad ready and go out and relieve the OP. I told him I would go but I would not be in charge. I said that was an E-5 sergeants position, to be a squad leader and run patrols, and if the Army wasn't going to make me an E-5, I wasn't going to lead a patrol out to the end of the ridge line or anywhere else. I didn't say I wouldn't go, I just said I was not going to take the responsibility for everybody in the squad if I wasn't going to get the rank.

I couldn't have cared less about the extra pay a sergeant got, but I did want the rank for two reasons. One, if I ever did get out of Vietnam I was going to have to spend seven months still in the Army back in the world. It would be a lot easier doing that time as an NCO (noncommissioned officer) than as an enlisted man. The other reason was that the men in our company got rank because of who they knew. I had heard there were only so many sergeant slots open at any one time, and when they came down, the clerks back in the rear got the rank for themselves and their friends. That left no sergeant slots for the grunts in the field who were actually doing the job. I know it seems like a small thing compared to getting shot, but we had so little and I wanted what was mine. Also, the guy in charge, the squad leader, was the guy the officers looked at if something went wrong. I didn't know it, but something was really going to go wrong on this patrol, and it was going to land on me.

The lieutenant didn't quite see eye to eye with me on my view of becoming a sergeant. He explained to me that he didn't care if I was a sergeant or was ever going to be a sergeant. What he did care about was that I collect my squad of men and go out there and relieve the OP so they could come back and eat. He explained further that I most definitely was in charge, whether I liked it or not, and if something went wrong he was holding me personally responsible. I remember him saying those exact words: "If something goes wrong on that patrol I am going to hold you personally responsible." I didn't like how he said that, but I shut up and got the men together and went out to relieve the OP. As I look back now, I think he was just trying to show his authority by making it clear that anything he said was the law and my opinion didn't mean shit.

The patrol was no big deal. It was late afternoon and all we had to do was walk out about a quarter of a mile, relieve the OP for four hours, and come back in when the next squad relieved us. There was little chance of us being attacked. There were two full infantry companies on the hill now, plus a motor company and an artillery battery. There were so many men on the hill that it was actually crowded.

On our way out to the OP, we met a group of combat engineers who had been setting up Bangalore Torpedoes to clear the brush. These were three-foot sections of tubing filled with explosives. The advantage of these tubes was that they could be stuck together end on end for as long as you wanted and all set off at the same time, clearing a path six feet wide on both sides for a total of a twelve-foot path. They were great for clearing a minefield or creating a fast chopper pad or, as in this case, clearing brush down to the ground for a good clear field of fire.

The engineers had to stop working as we went by. They were concerned we would trip over the tubes and set them all off, killing everybody, them and us. They screamed at us to be careful. I didn't think they were ever this far out in the field. They called themselves combat engineers but I don't think they were ever really in combat. If they had been, they would have known you didn't have to tell grunts to be careful around explosives on the trail—we knew.

We humped out the quarter mile and relieved the other squad. My friend "Coop" was in charge of the other squad. We had arrived at the company together and I liked him. It was no big deal—we said hi, took over the radio, and relieved them so they could go back in and eat. I heard the explosion and didn't think anything of it—the engineers finally setting off those Bangalore Torpedoes. One of the men in our squad was making a commotion and I left my position to see what was the matter. He said he had been watching the squad we relieved walk back to the perimeter and saw them walk into the area where the engineers were setting up the torpedoes just as the explosions went off.

We listened to the radio to hear any traffic about what had happened and if anybody was hurt. All we heard was a call for a dust-off. We couldn't just call for information; things didn't work like that. You had to assume the enemy was monitoring you at all times. Open conversation on a radio about something like this, an accident, would not be tolerated. We had to wait until we were relieved to find out what had happened to the squad. I was in shock. Guys were talking, asking whose fault it was. Shouldn't we have called in to let the company know the OP was coming in? They were saying it's not right, us killing our men, who was in charge anyway? Everybody knew who was in charge—me. They were all there for my confrontation with the lieutenant. They all heard him say, "If something goes wrong on that patrol, I am going to hold you personally responsible."

I couldn't look at anybody. Was I supposed to call in to the company that the relieved OP was coming in? Was that my job? Didn't they know they were coming in? I couldn't think straight. I went back to my machine gun position to hide from their looks. Now I am not sure if the looks were real or imagined, but I remember how I felt. I felt like I just killed my best friend, Coop.

We finally saw the dust-off come and go; there was only one chopper. I hoped that was a good sign. Maybe just a few guys got wounded and they would be OK. The four hours dragged on forever; I needed to know what had happened. Finally our relief came, and the news was worse than I thought. Everybody was killed. There was so little left of the bodies after the exploding tubes ripped through them that the small pieces of six men fit in one body bag. That's why one chopper and no chatter. There was nothing to say. The men were dead and no medic or doctor back at Chu Lai was going to change that. The only thing left to do was to fix the blame and dish out the punishment.

My mind raced. I still couldn't seem to understand if I had done anything wrong. Everybody else seemed to think so, or so I imagined. This wasn't like a firefight, no fight or flight. I couldn't get out of this one by shooting and running at the VC. The amount of guilt and shame I felt was going to suffocate me. I really needed to be told this was not my fault. I needed someone in authority to tell me, "Rob, you didn't kill your friends. You were in charge of the patrol but it was not your job to call in that the unit you relieved was coming back. Everyone should have known that." Of course, we did have their radio and they couldn't call in themselves.

It was pitch dark when we got back. The lieutenant was there to greet us, me. He told us we were relieved of duty tonight; another platoon was taking our place on the perimeter tonight, and we should find a place to sleep near the company command post tonight. Then he looked at me and said there was some battalion brass coming out at daylight to investigate the incident. He said I better get my story straight because someone was going to jail for this and it wasn't going to be him. That's not what I was hoping to hear just then. The good news was that Coop was not killed, although everyone else was. I went and talked to him. He was in a daze. He told me it was like God put his hands around him and protected him when the blast went off. He held out his hands to show me what he meant; he didn't get a scratch. Coop was from the South in the Bible Belt.

I was scared. I could see how this was going. This whole thing was going to be dumped on me. All those deaths were going to be blamed on me. I was going to jail for a long time, and instead of a hero's welcome coming home, my family would be reading about me in my hometown paper, how I caused the deaths of five good men. Well, I was a good man, too. I didn't sleep all night. My stomach hurt and my head kept spinning. I was sure I was going to be court-martialed and sent to Fort Leavenworth to do hard labor. I tried to see the good side; at least I would be getting out of the field. I stewed all night.

At first light, a chopper came in as promised and the pilot landed softly and turned off the engine. He was going to wait until the investigating officer was done and take him back to wherever he came from. Whoever this guy was, he was important enough to have his own chopper sit and wait for him. I started to feel worse, if that was possible. Nobody came near me or would look at me. When something like this happens, senseless deaths of good men, people need something or someone to blame. I was the guy who, not twelve hours before, was making all the noise about being in charge. "If I am going to do a sergeant's job, I want the rank." If I hadn't made such a fuss about being in charge, the lieutenant wouldn't have made such a point of putting me in charge, and putting me in the situation I was in now. I was the one they were blaming.

I eyed the colonel the battalion had sent out, as he walked by on his way to the command bunker. He was older, red faced, sort of fat, and not infantry. This guy had some crap ribbons on his starched uniform but no CIB (combat infantry badge). There was a little worm of a lieutenant following him, his lackey. Although I was mostly consumed by fear and guilt, I started to think about the engineers who detonated the blast. Why wasn't anybody looking at them? Weren't there some safety procedures before you blow up things? My fear started to turn into anger. I finally got called in to tell my version of what happened. Others had already talked to the colonel, but I couldn't get a sense of what was going on.

I entered the tent and started yelling at the colonel, saying it wasn't my fault that those men died, and I wasn't going to jail because of what someone else did. He looked up at me, startled, so I took another breath and started in again saying why it was not my fault and how I wasn't going to take the fall for some officer so they could blame an enlisted man. I figured a good offense was better than no defense. He raised his hand and stopped me in mid-sentence. In a very nice voice he told me that nobody was going to jail. He knew it was an accident and just needed to take statements from the people involved. He even consoled me on the loss of my friends.

I left the tent with a huge feeling of relief. Life went on in Black Death. The next firefight made us forget about the incident and I don't remember specifically what, but a new set of problems confronted me and I moved on.

MONSOONS

Somewhere along the line the monsoons started. Like Forrest Gump said, "It started raining one day and didn't stop for six months." Monsoons meant poor visibility; choppers flew less, and we went without. We went without food, supplies, gunships when we needed them, and anything else an army in the field needs that is only supplied by air. There were no roads. The gooks, on the other hand, weren't slowed down at all. Their supplies came in on the backs of their soldiers or laborers down the Ho Chi Minh Trail. As a matter of fact, their lives became easier because all their danger came from the air—choppers, jet fighters, jet bombers, surveillance planes, and anything else that flew.

Just to make my life a little more challenging I had jungle rot, sores that developed on my arms and legs in open cuts that I got from the elephant grass. What had been an inconvenience during the dry season now blossomed into full-blown, puss-oozing, open sores that never healed for the entire monsoon season. The medic on the fire support base LZ Center told me the penicillin that he had been giving me was starting to wear off because of overuse. He also said I had it so bad because of my very light Irish complexion. He suggested I try to keep my arms and feet dry or it could develop into something serious. I guess he didn't notice I lived outside in a jungle where it rained twenty-three hours a day, had only one set of clothes that were wet all the time, and slept on the ground in two or three inches of water. I guess he didn't notice that.

I remember one time when food supplies got real low. We didn't get our small re-supply and the day our main re-supply was due, the weather made it impossible to fly. A lot of guys were out of food, but because I was bigger than most I could carry more food in my rucksack. I kept my extra food a secret and would eat it on my guard duty at night. I very carefully opened my stash, making sure nobody heard the slightest metallic sound of P-38 (can opener) and can. It wasn't like I had a lot to eat, or anything really good like a can of peaches, but I had a few items that had been picked over time and time again and had gotten to the bottom on my pack. I remember finding a small can of peanut butter that I had not seen before, tucked underneath some C-4 plastic explosives. I couldn't wait until my turn for guard duty. I slowly opened the can. It held about one ounce of peanut butter, which I slowly ate with my finger because a spoon might make some noise. If I made any noise my friends would know I was holding back food and they would not like me, which sounds silly now but meant so much then.

We didn't move for a couple of days because the CO didn't think his men had the strength to be humping up and down hills all day without food. It had been two days since we had missed our re-supply and we were out of food, actually we had been out of food before the choppers were scheduled to re-supply us, now we were desperate.

We were slowly starving to death, and like most Americans I had never know hunger like this. I don't mean like missing a few meals and having some hunger pains, I am talking about feeling your body feeding on it self and hearing a voice inside you, talking above the dull pain in the base of your skull telling you if you don't eat you will die, that kind of hunger.

The captain finally passed around the word for everybody in the platoon to take turns sending out patrols to scavenge for food. He said to find any village or hooch area you could, take anything you found to eat, and come back and let the next group go out. I made sure I went out on the first patrol. We quickly came to a small hooch area. I went inside and saw a young woman squatting down over a cook fire with two young children by her side. It was raining outside and wasn't much drier inside the hooch. She was cooking something in a black pot that smelled awful—I mean, it's hard to describe how bad this crap smelled. There were fifty flies buzzing around the pot. I grabbed the pot off its hook and went outside and ate it, reaching in the pot and pulling out small handfuls and stuffing them in my mouth. It actually tasted worse than it smelled.

OPEN MESS

A few weeks later my friend Peter and I somehow got to go back to Chu Lai, our division's base camp. While we were there we saw a sign that said "Open Mess." In the Army, an open mess is a mess hall where military personnel of any rank can eat. This was a stroke of luck. We looked in and saw they were still serving breakfast. We probably didn't look too good. It was still monsoon season and our clothes looked like we had just taken a mud bath. We got in line and grabbed a tray.

There was hardly any line and the cooks who were serving the meal looked at us strangely. I thought at first it might be the jungle rot, which had extended to my face, but this was an Air Force mess hall and they probably didn't get a lot of grunts. As the cooks put the food on our trays, they asked if we wanted more. This was unheard of in our world, so of course we had them put as much food on our trays as they could hold. The cooks found this amusing and piled the trays to overflowing, until the food was dropping off the trays and falling onto the floor.

We were in heaven. It had been a real long time since we had a meal like this and we grabbed a table and started eating. It had not occurred to us to pick up any silverware, grunts always carried a plastic spoon in their pockets in case an opportunity came along to eat. We bent low over the trays, pushing the food into our mouths. The rule in the field was to eat as fast as you could. Anything could happen and it was easy to miss out on a meal if you took too much time. We ate in silence while looking up, scanning the room for possible danger. Talking could wait until later; this was eating time.

I could see we were drawing a lot of attention and the room was starting to buzz. These Air Force guys really lived good. This place was beautiful and everybody looked so clean and fresh. One female officer, I had no idea what the stuff on her uniform meant so I didn't know her rank, looked like she was really getting upset and called over the top mess sergeant. She was too far away to hear, but she was reading him the riot act and she was stabbing her finger in the air in our direction. The mess sergeant was a lifer, old and sort of fat. He looked at us—we were still stuffing food in our mouths as fast as we could—and hesitated. He said something back to the woman officer that threw her into a fit. She started on him again and before she finished talking he started to slowly walk toward us. He came up to our table almost apologetically and told us that this was an Air Force officers' mess hall and we would have to leave. We didn't move; we just looked up at him and kept on eating. He looked back at the lady, shrugged, and put his hand on Peter's shoulder saying, "Come on now, let's not cause a scene. You will have to go."

Peter sprang up, grabbing the hair on the back of the mess sergeant's head with one hand and taking his .45-caliber pistol out of his holster with the other hand. He put the gun in the mess sergeant's face and forced the muzzle into his mouth. The entire mess hall froze. Nobody moved or said a word. Peter grunted to the mess sergeant to start moving toward the door. I got up, grabbing both trays and our M-16s, and followed Peter and the sergeant to the door. At the door, Peter shoved the mess sergeant to the floor and we ran out. I handed Peter his tray and rifle and we ran off laughing in the rain. We found a large storm drain that ran under the road. We had to walk through a few feet of water, but the big pipe made a nice place for us to finish our meal. We heard jeeps driving around, probably looking for us. It was lucky for those Air Force pukes they didn't find us. We would have killed them in a heartbeat and then gone out looking for lunch.

JOB ON THE HILL

I remember a month or so later Peter got a job up on "The Hill," as we called it. The Hill was a fire support base called LZ Center that housed a battery of artillery and a mortar company. Around the perimeter of the hill was a series of bunkers where an infantry company would pull a week on duty, protecting the hill. For the artillery and mortar guys, this was the field; they felt they were in harm's way. They felt they lived like animals, sleeping in damp underground bunkers each night and eating the same old slop the mess hall served each day and who knows, if the morning resupply ship didn't come they might have to eat C-rations. They talked like the VC were going to run up the hill and start shooting their AK-47s at any minute. Of course, compared to the REMFs (rear-echelon mother fuckers) at Chu Lai, they did live like animals.

To us, the hill was a great place to be. You got to sleep in nice dry bunkers that were safe because they were underground. You got to eat hot chow, served three times a day, and if the choppers couldn't get in, there were literally tons of C-rations there to eat, so you would never run out of food. On top of that, the gooks were so far away down in the valley you felt as safe as anyone could be, and still be in Vietnam.

Now to get a permanent job on The Hill was the ultimate dream come true. I think Peter got pulled out of the field because he was nuts. Everybody was pushed to the edge, but Peter was nuts before he came to Vietnam, so I think for the good of the company our lieutenant had him put on The Hill. They had him digging holes and building new bunkers with an engineering outfit.

One of the times I was able to get out of the field, I had to go to Chu Lai for something and I stayed a night on The Hill on my way back. This was great because I now knew some guys there, and I would have a nice place to stay and we could get some beer and have sort of a party. When I say a nice place to stay and a party, I mean Peter could probably buy us a case of warm beer for a month's pay and we could find a corner in an ammo bunker or some supply hut and we could drink the beer and fall asleep where we were sitting.

I guess Peter was feeling guilty about him being up on The Hill, and me still slugging it out in the bush. In his pea-brain little mind he came up with a plan to solve his problem of guilt and my problem of still being in a rifle company. I'll give Peter this; he was direct and loyal. If he didn't like you he would let you know, no games or back stabbing. If he didn't like you, stay out of his way or you were going to wish you did. Peter was from the Ozarks—I'm not sure how far back in the hills his family came from, but the idea of wearing shoes seemed new to him. On the other hand, if he did like you he was your friend, and in his mind friends took care of each other.

I was hoping that now he was up on The Hill, maybe he could put in a good word for me with someone and get me a job there, and I had told him so. Looking back now, I see what a childish, naive thought that was. I didn't have a clue how these things worked and the politics involved in getting a cushy job like his, but at the time I would have tried anything. Even my friend Peter knew—the guy's too crazy to be in an infantry company because he might hurt the other men, men armed to the teeth who killed gooks on a daily basis—this guy knew I had no chance of getting out of the field without a dust-off.

So Peter came up with a plan to get his friend, me, out of the field before some VC did. Like Peter, his plan was direct and simple. The next time he saw me he would get me drunk, with some beer he hid away just for the occasion, and when I was passed out on the floor he would smash my foot with a sledgehammer he had hidden away with the beer. He figured if I couldn't walk they would have to let me out. Now this plan wasn't without some merits. We spent a lot of time on hot nights in our foxholes trying to figure out some way to get out of the madness. The obvious way was to shoot yourself in the foot, but the medics and doctors were trained to look for this kind of self-inflicted wound and we had all heard horror stories of guys who tried and either ended up in jail at Fort Leavenworth for twenty years of hard labor, or healed up and got put back in a rifle company after spending time in LBJ with their time on freeze until they got back to the field. These were not idle threats made by the Army. They were good at what they did, and one thing they knew how to do was to keep infantrymen in the field and not let them out because they hurt themselves. Otherwise, everybody would shoot himself and get out of the field, on both sides.

Then there was the question of where exactly you would shoot yourself, or have your buddy shoot you, in the foot. I remember taking off our shoes and looking at our feet to see where would be a good place for a bullet to pass through, causing just enough damage to get you home, but not enough to make you a permanent gimp (I remembered our CO's warning at Tiger Land). Then the conversation would wander to other parts of the anatomy, maybe a bullet through an arm or upper thigh. The problem was always the same. Guys were shot all the time. They would get dusted off, get patched up at the hospital, and come back out in a few weeks or months, whatever it took to keep experienced troops in the field. The same skills that kept you alive in the field were the skills that the Army needed, so they would always patch you up and put you back. The only way out was "the head or the heart." This was a saying—unless you got shot in the head or the heart, you were coming back.

When I first got to Black Death, there was a company rule: if you got shot and came back you would get a job in the rear or on The Hill. Then the rule changed to: if you got shot twice, the second time you would get a job in the rear or on The Hill. Then the rule changed to three times. After I had been there six months the rule got thrown out altogether. My assistant gunner, J.J. Jones from South Carolina, got shot three separate times. Once, three of us were crouched down in a ditch so close we were touching. J.J. got shot in the arm and I felt the bullet. I had to look to see which one of us got shot. He looked, too; it was a black ugly wound but he didn't seem to mind much. I looked over at the other guy, I can never remember his name, and saw a bullet go through his face. My slow motion was working really well that day and I can still see the bullet coming through the air, going through his cheek and out his mouth. I see it now, thirty years later, as clear as then. Both those guys were back in a few weeks.

So Peter's plan was workable. Once my foot was smashed, he would tell everybody it was his fault, some construction mishap, and I would go home. He must have put a lot of thought into it. He was real happy to see me when I just showed up one day. He got the beer and we went to his bunker to drink it. I thought nothing of the sledgehammer he was carrying, a common tool in the unit he now worked in. Guilt is a strong emotion. I guess the same guilt that made him feel bad because he was out of the field and I wasn't, made him drink faster and harder than I did. I felt like I was on vacation and wanted to take my time, savor the moment.

Peter got drunk and while we were sitting there he grabbed the sledgehammer and with all his strength brought it over his head and slammed it down toward my right foot. I pulled my foot out of the way just in time and the hammer hit the floor like thunder. I looked at him, astonished. He broke down crying, telling me his whole plan, including his discussion with a medic on The Hill who had some formal training at a medical school. The medic assured him the proper blow, struck on the upper portion of the front of the foot, near the ankle, would get me sent home. Peter apologized for getting drunk and striking too early, and suggested we keep drinking and all my problems would be over in the morning. Peter was a strong guy. I could see him smashing my foot in my sleep, hitting me a few extra times for good measure. I declined, and shortly after excused myself to go take a leak. I left the bunker and found another place to sleep—someplace he couldn't find if he came looking after a few more beers. I was touched by his caring, though; it meant a lot to me.

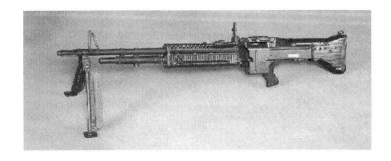

This is the M-60 Machine Gun that I lugged around the jungle for eight months as a machine gunner. The other four months I was a rifleman and I carried an M-16 rifle or an M-79 grenade launcher

THE BIG BLUE

Our company was sent on a mission to find and assault an NVA stronghold that was high up in a mountain range across the Big Blue, a large river running along the edge of our AO. It was a very rugged area, uninhabited by anything but monkeys and tigers and snakes. It was decided that we would be picked up by choppers and dropped off about five miles from the river. That way, Viet Cong lookouts couldn't tell where we were going because the sound and the sight of the choppers would announce our arrival wherever we landed.

Once we were on the ground and moving, it would be much harder for them to keep track of our location and it would be very hard for them to tell where we were going. It was very important to us to keep our attack on the NVA stronghold a surprise. We didn't know the troop size of the NVA and we would be attacking a secured position dug into the top of a mountain. That meant we would be attacking underground bunkers from a downhill position. The only advantage we had was surprise.

The choppers came in at sunrise. As always they came in waves, four choppers at a time, in a diamond pattern. The four company machine guns always were in the first wave, one machine gun and its crew per chopper. After we lifted off, a second wave of four choppers landed and picked up riflemen to support the machine guns if the drop zone was hot. Then the two waves of choppers flew to the drop-off location. As we approached the drop-off position the first wave, the wave I was on with the machine guns, slowly descended to an open field for the landing.

The idea was for all four choppers to land at the same time. If there were hostile troops waiting for us at the landing zone, we wanted four targets for them to shoot at. If the choppers landed one at a time, all the enemy fire could be concentrated on first one chopper and then the next, and they would kill us one chopper at a time. By landing together we would break up their fire concentration and have a much better chance of getting off the chopper and returning fire. The second wave always held off, flying high above us out of range. That way, if there was a hot landing they could come in to support us at the drop-off zone after our choppers got airborne and left, or they could land at a different drop-off zone away from the firefight, unload the choppers in relative safety, and come back to support us. Of course, if the drop zone was too hot and all four choppers got shot down, with us in them, the second wave might just turn around and go back to the company and leave us there. The mission was what was important, not the individual. I didn't like being in the first wave.

The drop zone was cold (no enemy fire) and we landed and unloaded without incident. After the two waves of choppers landed and dropped us off, they returned to the company and ferried the rest of them to our location. In about forty-five minutes the whole company had arrived at the drop zone and we were on our way to the Big Blue, the first objective of the mission.

At first the walking was easy; there were farms and rice paddies and trails. As we got closer to the river, the trail petered out and we had to push through the jungle, making our own path as we moved. Finally the jungle got so thick the point squad bogged down and we were hardly moving. My platoon was the second platoon in line, so out of three platoons we were in the middle, a good safe place to be. The temperature was starting to rise and the bugs were starting to bite. We would move a few feet, then stop and wait. We would have to stand there sweating until we moved again, sometimes for ten minutes or more. You couldn't talk, sit down, or take your pack off. You had to just stand still not making a sound, sweating, waiting until you could move again.

I carried the machine gun on my shoulder. I would fold a green towel and place it on my shoulder under the machine gun to pad the weight. The machine gun weighed about twenty-three pounds in the morning; by sundown it seemed to weigh about eight hundred. I also wore a rucksack with all my food, water, and any other supplies in it, and a pistol belt with the pistol and extra ammo clips, smoke grenades, and anti-personnel grenades. When you were standing still you noticed the weight more. It just sat there, pulling on your shoulders. You stood there thinking how miserable you were, and how nice it would be to go home and drink beer and be with girls. On top of everything else was the machine gun ammo. It was in belts of one hundred rounds that were worn crisscross over your shoulders, two belts one way and two belts the other way, for a total of four hundred rounds. I looked like the pictures I had seen of a Mexican bandito or Poncho Villa without the horse. The ammo had to be worn on the outside so that if you were killed the ammo could be ripped off your body. It was hard to move dead weight. The mission was what was important, not the individual.

I had to take the machine gun off my shoulder each time we stopped, placing it on the ground slowly so it wouldn't make any noise, butt first so it was standing on end with the muzzle facing up. I would lean over and rest my arms on the legs of the gun. With my head hanging down, waiting, I would be looking straight down into the barrel. I could see the copper tip of the bullet chambered in the machine gun. The gun could so easily have misfired and gone off, taking my head with it. I didn't see how I was going to keep this up for another nine months, going from one firefight to another, without getting killed. Standing there in the stifling heat, waiting for the column to move a few feet and stopping again, was nerve-racking. It gave you too much time to think, too much time to realize how miserable you were, with the jungle reaching out and trying to tear your skin off with its thorns. Every time I put the gun down or picked it up, a vine would grab the barrel or the belt of ammo sticking out, and I would have to untangle the vines before I could move.

Of course, if this was the hardest part of the mission it would have been bearable, but this was only the beginning. We still had to get to the river, somehow cross the river without drowning, then climb a mountain range for a couple of days. Our reward for doing all that was to attack a secured NVA stronghold with an unknown strength. Before and during the attack there would be a lot of air support—jet fighters, helicopters, gun ships, and anything else our captain would ask for. The one thing we couldn't get was more troops; the jungle was too thick and choppers couldn't land. We were getting into what is called a triple-canopy jungle. In a triple-canopy forest there is one set of trees about forty high that covers the entire forest floor, then another set of trees that grows about twenty feet above the first layer. As the name implies, there is a third canopy, the thickest because of its exposure to sunlight, which covers everything under it. There was no way to land a chopper in that jungle.

After all the air support was over, we were going to have to move in on that NVA camp and overrun it by ourselves—no backup, no calling in more infantry to help us, no choppers to pull us out if it got too hot. The only way out of that jungle was to take the top of the hill, where the NVA were, or go back the way we came, three days marching. On the top of the mountain, the jungle was much thinner because the trees couldn't get as much water, it ran off because of the slope, and an LZ could be cut with detonating cord. Once you had an LZ, you could have choppers.

The point squad finally realized they couldn't push through the brush anymore so they found a stream to follow, figuring it would lead them to the river. We marched down the middle of the stream toward the river; it got deeper with each step. After a while, the stream spread out wide and became a swamp. The stinking swamp water got up to our waists and kept getting deeper, but there was no way to get to dry land except back the way we came, and that was not an option. The slimy green swamp water finally got up to our shoulders and only our heads were above water. We held our weapons up above our heads to keep them dry, but it was hard. Eventually the point squad guided us to some dry land and then to the bank of the Big Blue. The river was about one hundred yards wide and it moved pretty fast. We somehow had to cross it.

Our first sergeant was quite resourceful. He came up with a plan for us to cross the river in force, in case the gooks were on the other side waiting for us. He had us use our machetes to cut down bamboo trees to use as poles. Then we blew up our air mattresses and took the shoelaces out of our boots. We tied the bamboo poles and air mattresses together making rafts, with four mattresses to a raft. I thought it was a great idea. He had us make four rafts and spread them out on the riverbank. We had to keep plenty of room between rafts, again to split up the enemy fire if they were waiting for us. There was a heated discussion as to who should go over on the first rafts. Should it be the four machine guns like in the choppers, putting our best foot forward, or should riflemen go on the first wave, letting the four machine guns stay on our side of the river, so they could be used for cover fire if the rafts were ambushed? Personally, I voted for the machine guns to stay on our side of the river and be used for cover fire. Unfortunately, this was not a democracy and my vote didn't count. The machine guns were to go over first.

We had to take off all of our clothes so we could swim more easily as we pushed the raft across the river. I didn't mind the swimming part; I was a good swimmer. I just didn't like being naked in front of everybody. We piled all our equipment, rucksacks and stuff, on the rafts and put the machine guns on top of the equipment to get a better angle if we had to fire them. After all four rafts were loaded and ready, we waited for the signal to start. It was important we all stayed in a line to cross the river. Getting offline would make it easier to be picked off by enemy fire, and harder to be protected by cover fire. The first sergeant realized we couldn't go straight across because of the current, so he sent a platoon downstream one hundred yards, figuring that was where we would hit the other side. The signal came to kick off and we started.

The plan was a good one, but our first sergeant was an Army man, not a Navy man. The rafts didn't track as we expected and the current twisted us all up. No amount of kicking in the water behind the rafts could keep us straight. We did get to the other side, but it wasn't orderly. There were no gooks and no enemy fire. After we unloaded all the equipment on the other riverbank, one of us had to bring the raft back so the rest of the company could start coming over. It took about three hours for the whole company (about one hundred men) to cross the river and get ready to start marching again. I had made the swim three times. I liked swimming and once you got the hang of it, the rafts worked quite well, but I was exhausted and I should never have volunteered to bring the raft back twice. I forgot the basic rule of the Army enlisted man—never volunteer, for anything. It wouldn't happen again. We lost one man; apparently he got caught in the current and was swept downstream. We never found his body.

We started marching again. I felt clean—baths were rare—but everything I had was soaking wet. That made everything heavier, and all my clothes stuck to my body and made it harder to walk and move. In that heat and humidity nothing was going to dry out soon. It didn't take long before the point squad got bogged down again and the same walk-a-few-feet-and-then-wait started up. Too much time to think.

We inched our way up the first hill; it took hours. At the top of the hill the jungle thinned out a bit and you could see forward. All I saw was another hill to climb, this one much higher and steeper. We kept moving this way until it got dark, when we tried to form a perimeter. It was hard because there was no open space and you could only see a few feet. The next morning we started again at sun up.

We marched the whole next day, jungle crawling to the top of one hill only to find another hill waiting for us to climb. When darkness came the second night, we didn't even bother to try to set up a perimeter. We just stopped in our tracks and went to sleep. We didn't even set up guard duty or lookouts. We were halfway up the main mountain and the jungle was so thick even the VC couldn't get to us without making a lot of noise. I remember not even being able to lie down on the ground; the vines were so thick and twisted, we lay on them like hammocks.

I had started to feel bad about noon on the second day from the water I had been drinking. I could tell the water was bad when I filled my canteens that morning, but we didn't get a chance to find clear water and the only thing worse than bad water was no water at all. I know everybody thinks they know what it's like to be thirsty, but until you have spent twenty-four hours or more in tropical heat and humidity at hard labor without water, thirsty means your mouth is sort of dry. The stream I got it from, that we marched through, was fast moving, but the water was green and I knew better than to drink it. I had hoped to find better water farther ahead on the trail, but we were too high in the mountains and there were no streams.

When I woke up that morning my stomach was flipping. I started to get diarrhea during the first couple of hours on the trail and I had to play catch-up. When I stopped to relieve myself, I got off the trail for some privacy and then had to catch up to where my spot was in the procession. By the time I started throwing up, I was too weak to carry the machine gun and I had to change off with my assistant gunner. I took his M-16, which was much lighter and a lot easier to move around. I had gotten dysentery from the bad water and it was going to get a lot worse before it got better. I finally got too weak to keep moving and lay down beside the column of troops moving to the impending battle at the top of the hill.

Someone called ahead on the radio to my platoon sergeant and he came back with the medic. The medic confirmed I was too sick to move on. As the sergeant took all my food and ammo and anything else they could use from my pack, he told me to crawl off into the jungle and hide until I felt better and could move. He suggested I could tell what was happening in the battle by the air traffic. He told me if things went bad, to try to make it back to the LZ but don't go the way we came, use a different route. He said if we secure the hilltop make sure you call out very loud so you don't take friendly fire. He did leave me my .45-caliber pistol. He even gave me an extra clip of his own. I appreciated that. Where he was going he might really need that extra clip.

As I write this now, thirty years later, I see in movies and TV shows about units in the Army having the motto "Leave no man behind." If our unit had a motto it would have been "Keep up, asshole, or we will leave you behind." They left me in a New York minute. It was the only reasonable thing to do. They were heading into what could be a very dangerous battle. Any energy wasted on a sick man would only take away from the resources of the company and not help complete the mission. The mission is what counted, not the individual.

What the sergeant meant when he said I could tell how things were going by the air traffic was that I was close enough to the hilltop to hear what type of airships were flying over and what they were doing. If I kept hearing jets dropping bombs, not just after the initial attack but later, things would be going bad. That would mean the NVA was dug in good. I would expect to hear the jets let up so the infantry could attack on the ground and try to overrun the compound. If the jets started in again or I could hear Cobra gunships, that meant the attack was repelled and air support would be brought back in. This time the airships would have more accurate target information. The infantry would be able to identify the locations of the dug-in bunkers because the NVA would have given away their location by shooting and killing GIs. After the second bombardment, the infantry would move in again. Hopefully, those bunkers and the men inside would have been destroyed by the airships. If they weren't destroyed, or new ones popped up that hadn't shown themselves in the first assault, their positions would be noted and passed along to the airships.

What would happen is this: an infantry unit, maybe one pinned down by fire, would pop smoke (throw a smoke grenade). The guy with the radio would ask the aircraft if he saw the smoke. When the aircraft said he saw the smoke, the guy on the ground would ask the pilot what color smoke he saw. If the pilot said he saw the correct color smoke, the guy on the ground would tell the pilot the location of the ground units from the smoke—we are one hundred yards south from the smoke. Then he would tell the pilot the position of the enemy bunker—75 yards north of the smoke. After the airship made its run, the guy on the ground could adjust the next run by telling the pilot to drop one hundred feet, or west two hundred feet. Hopefully, on the next run the bunker would be destroyed. The problem was, the little gook bastards were smart. They knew what was going to happen so they dug in really deep, maybe twenty feet or more from the entrance to the bunker. When you were sure they had to be dead—the whole place was blown up and it was just a big open hole in the ground—the yellow bastards were still there when you assaulted again. These guys didn't die easily.

So there I was, lying in the fetal position, hiding in the jungle, trying to listen to the air traffic so I could tell what was going on. It seemed like a long time before I heard anything. I kept falling asleep so I lost track of time, but it was taking forever. By staying still and resting I seemed to feel a little better. The stomach spasms seemed to slow down, and when they came they were not as bad. I was trying to think of what to do. Should I try to get closer to the battle so I could tell what was going on, or start to back down the hill in case the battle went bad and I had to make my way back across the LZ we came in on two days before? I stayed put. I wasn't sure if I felt better because the dysentery had run its course or I was just so relieved I didn't have to be in this battle. Either way, I felt lucky to be where I was.

It was late afternoon when I heard the jets. The bombing runs came and went. I held my breath, waiting to hear what sounds would come next. I heard choppers, but I couldn't tell if they were Cobra gunships or regular slicks. If they were regular slicks that would mean they were resupply ships and the battle was over. It seemed too soon for everything to be over. I closed my eyes and strained to hear what was going on. I thought I could hear choppers landing and taking off again. If that was true, everything was good. Slicks don't land in the middle of battles. Then I remembered that medivacs do. But I couldn't hear any small arms fire or any shooting at all. We were probably too far out in the boondocks for an artillery battery to reach us, but if those were medivacs there would be M-16s and AK-47s going off, and there weren't.

The sun was setting and I had to move if I wasn't going to stay where I was all night. I stood up and started up the way the company had gone. I was shaky and had a wobble but the closer I got to the hilltop, the surer I was those were resupply ships landing; I was sure it was over. I started yelling out, "Man coming in," way before anybody could hear me. I did not want to get shot by some green seed, new to the company and a danger to himself and anyone around him. My call was finally answered. A voice said, "Come ahead," and I walked into the company perimeter.

The resupply ships had brought in hot chow, mail, and a beer and soda ration. We each got two cans of soda or beer with our big resupply every four days, weather permitting. I could see everybody wolfing down their hot chow and their drinks. I found my machine gun squad's position on the perimeter and asked what happened. My assistant gunner answered with a full mouth, "The gooks were gone when we got here. Want some hot chow?" That was it—no gooks, no battle. I couldn't look at the food without getting sick. A few days later we got choppered off the mountaintop and went on to our next mission.

This place could kill you without the enemy even being there.

OBSERVATION POST

In our AO (area of operation), which was all high hills and low valleys, we had three fire support bases called LZ East, LZ Center, and LZ West. They looked like mountains to me, but it only took three or four hours to hike up any one of them, so they called them hills. The fire support bases were set up in a triangle. That way, if one base was attacked the other two could help by firing their artillery and mortars at the sides of the hill where the enemy was. These fire support bases also acted as fire support for the rifle companies, down in the valleys, looking for VC and NVA. Each hill had two permanent Ops (observation post). A permanent observation post was a hill not far from the fire support base that had about four men all the time. From the vantage point of the observation post they could observe the valleys below and call in artillery attacks or air strikes if they saw movement on the enemy trails. Whichever rifle company was on the hill at the time would have to man these observation posts.

I didn't buy the story that the purpose of the observation post was to watch the valleys below; they didn't have any better view of the trails than the fire support bases had. Besides, we all knew gooks didn't move during the day, they moved at night. The gooks could move ten thousand men through those valleys at night and no one from the OP could see them or hear them. What all the OPs did have, though, was a good view of the fire support bases. I figured the real reason for the permanent OPs was to act as warning devices. I had spent a lot of time thinking about the bigger picture, not just what was going on in my platoon or company. I tried to get an idea of what was happening in the whole AO. I could not have cared less about the overall political picture of the Vietnam War, but whatever went on in that maze of hills and valleys called our area of operation was going to affect me.

After a considerable amount of time spent thinking about the fire support base system and the permanent OPs, I came up with a few undisputed facts. First, gooks weren't stupid, especially when it came to military tactics. The main military tactic I had seen them use was to work at night, getting as close to the GI defense position as possible, as soon as possible. This way if they got in fast and close, the GIs couldn't use their advanced technology, artillery, and air support without hitting themselves. The gooks would overrun the GI defensive position, take what prisoners they wanted to interrogate later, and kill the rest. Then they would split up and blend back into the jungle, with a rallying point miles away. By splitting up they never gave the gun ships and jets a large target, which could be wiped out easily.

To get back to my point about the OPs: because the gooks weren't stupid, they would never attack just one hill; they would attack all three fire support bases at once. This way all the bases would be busy defending themselves and not be able to defend each other. If one of the bases was overrun, the gooks could turn that base's artillery and mortars on the other hills and they all might fall like dominoes. In order to orchestrate such a maneuver, the NVA would need good observation of all three hills to direct the operation. We were required to call in every hour so that if the permanent OP was overrun, the officers on the hills would know something was going on and raise up their defenses, saving their own asses. So I figured the permanent OPs were there as warning systems, sacrificial lambs waiting for the slaughter. If we didn't call in, or they heard us screaming for help, they would know something was happening.

One time when our company was up on the hill, our squad was chosen to go out on one of those four-day OPs. I had been on them before, just four men out on a hilltop for four days. The gooks knew where we were. They could come up there any time they wanted and overrun us. There was no way four men could stop them. I viewed being on those OPs like playing musical chairs. When the music stopped and you were on the OP, you lost.

We got ready for the four-day mission by packing as much food and water as possible. Once the chopper dropped us off on the hilltop, we just stayed in the area, waiting to be picked up in four days or be overrun and killed. Either way, there was no reason not to be comfortable, so we brought as much with us as possible. You didn't have to carry it anywhere. This guy "Big John" and I were in charge. We had two newer guys with us, but we were the old men. There wasn't anything to be in charge of; once on the hill you just sat there waiting, alternating the guard while the other three guys slept or ate or talked or read something. During our briefing for the four-day mission, the lieutenant talking to us told us the last team was pulled out the day before, early, I forget why. The important point to us was that the hilltop had been empty for almost twenty-four hours and there was no way to tell what or who would be there to greet us. He said they had sent some flybys over the hilltop to see if anybody was there and the choppers didn't report any activity. He told us they didn't expect any trouble but they would be on alert when we got off the slick, and to call in our situation as soon as possible. Sitting there listening to that briefing assured me, being an officer, that this lieutenant probably had never even been to that hilltop or even been on a four-day OP.

We waited on the chopper pad for the slick. When the slick landed, the two new guys got in the middle and Big John and I got on each side door. That way we would be the first out the door. The slick rose up and sort of dropped off the hill, gaining air speed so it could get lift. No matter how many times I watched them fly, it thrilled me. Whenever I rode in one I got goose bumps from the excitement. Even when we went on a CA (combat assault) I loved the way they made me feel. A combat assault was a troop movement of company size or more.

As much as I loved looking at and riding in helicopters, the crews were a different story. When these slicks came in to land and pick you up, you weren't introduced all around to the pilots and the door gunners. They were just anonymous men, crewing a chopper, delivering you from point A to point B. They always had on those damn helmets with the black sun visors that didn't let you see their eyes, but you could see their jaws moving while they talked. And they always seemed to be talking to each other. Of course, everything was so loud you couldn't hear anyway, but you could see them talking and it felt to me like there was some private joke going on. I always felt they were talking about their cargo—us—and how they could dispose of it as soon as possible.

So when you went on a CA you just jumped in the chopper and sat there. The chopper crew would have their little chat, lasting only a few seconds, and then take off, heading to the LZ. Landing in the LZ was a different story. Choppers don't just come down out of the sky like an elevator. They have to come in low, losing air speed and lift at the same time, then sort of flare up and hover for a short while, and land so the troops can be safely discharged from the aircraft. When all the troops are off safe and clear, they can power up and take off. I am sure it must say something like that in some helicopter manual somewhere, but that's not how it worked. These guys wanted you out as soon as possible, and they didn't seem to think landing was a prerequisite to dumping out the troops. They would throw you out at one hundred feet at a speed of eighty miles per hour if they could get away with it. As graceful as these machines were in the air, when they landed they were slow and became easy targets for anybody waiting to knock them out of the air—big bullet magnets.

We wanted to get away from the slick as soon as possible, too, but getting thrown out at ten or fifteen feet was too high. With a full pack you were top heavy, and sometimes you landed on your head or on your back, lying there like a turtle trying to get up. The door gunners would grab the guy closest to the door and push him out, just as he was trying to jump. There you were, teetering on the edge of an aircraft that's moving up and down and side to side all at the same time, trying to get your timing so you can jump and land on your feet and start running, and some door gunner grabs you by your pack and pushes you out. See, that's what they were talking about in their little private conversations—when to throw us out. This didn't happen when a chopper came in for a re-supply, or some ordinary transport with a secure LZ, but from every combat assault I was ever on, I was thrown out like yesterday's trash.

When Big John and I were going out on that four-day mission, we were loaded down with supplies as heavily as I'd ever been. The chopper flew out over the valley and headed toward our hilltop destination. It wasn't that far by air; you could easily see the hill where we were going from LZ Center. The chopper flew over the landing area and pulled away. The pilot went down a valley and circled; something seemed to be wrong. The door gunner motioned me to let him speak in my ear. He yelled there was some movement on top of the hill at the primary LZ so we were going to circle around and come in at one of the secondary LZs. My first thought was that I felt special because one of the crew was even talking to me, letting me know what was going on. My second thought was that we weren't prepared to go into an assault.

We were all loaded down for a four-day sit and wait. My machine gun wasn't even loaded. There was no need; the belt of ammo would just be flopping around, maybe get damaged. Our mission was to sit there on that hilltop, fat and happy like a tethered goat, waiting for the lion to come and eat us. When the firebase heard our screams, our job was done. Our mission was not to assault a hilltop, with possible VC defensive positions, with four men.

Of course, our opinion wasn't asked for, so the chopper came around to the backside of the hill, away from the top of the hill where they saw the movement. I looked over at Big John. It was way too loud to talk, but his eyes told me he was thinking the same thing. We both moved out farther from the doors, standing up on the slicks (the bottom rails the helicopter lands on). We were trying to get in a good position to jump off the helicopter. This wasn't going to be the usual cakewalk that it should have been; we were trying to get ready for anything. The helicopter couldn't seem to get positioned right. It kept coming in to land, and backing off. There were trees in the way and the side of the hill was steep, not a good place to land.

At this point, Big John and I were wired. We were hanging out of the helicopter on either side, waiting for an opportunity to jump; there was no way it could land. The helicopter was just hovering there, trying to get a good position to let us off, when the side of the hill came under me. The door gunner grabbed my pack, but before he had a chance to push me out of the helicopter and send me tumbling down the hill, I jumped. When I jumped, the helicopter went off balance and tried to turn over. To offset the helicopter's off balance, the helicopter pilot compensated and brought the chopper back, right side up. As it came right side up again it kept going, and the blade hit the ground on the side of the hill a foot above my head. As I watched the helicopter from the hillside, it started to wobble around and seemed to fall off the hill, heading down to the valley below. I watched as it gained air speed and stability and circled back and did a flyover, to see what happened to me, I assumed. I had landed mostly on my feet and fell forward the way I wanted to. It had been a long fall but I was all right. As I lay there I looked at where the chopper blade had hit the ground, right above my head. Too much was happening at the same time and I couldn't think about that now.

After the helicopter flew over me it passed the top of the hill and went out of sight. I listened to the sound of its engines until the sound grew quieter and I could tell it had gone. I lay there taking stock of my position. I was alive and not injured, but alone. I had no radio—that was still in the helicopter—no way to communicate with anyone. There might be gooks on top of the hill but I had no way of knowing. I did have plenty of food and water, though. I took my pack off and waited. After about twenty minutes I realized nothing was going to happen with me sitting there. I couldn't call in for instructions without a radio. A helicopter couldn't come and pick me up because it couldn't land. I was going to have to go up to the hilltop. I didn't think there was anybody there, except maybe some local VC who realized no GIs were there and were scavenging for food or lost ammo or anything else that might have been left. I was sure if that were the case we would have scared them off with the chopper. I left my rucksack and went on top and waited for the chopper to come back with the rest of my team.

About half an hour later the chopper finally showed up. I popped smoke (threw out a colored smoke grenade) to show the pilot my position and the wind direction. It landed and the other three men got out of the chopper. After the chopper left and we could talk, Big John started pointing at me and laughing. He kept laughing and giggling saying, "Boy that chopper pilot was mad at you." Then he would go into another fit of laughter, holding his sides and pointing at me some more. We were on a mission with nothing to do, and four days to do it in. I could tell he was going to stretch this out as long as possible. I asked why the pilot was mad at me, and this brought more laughter and finger pointing. When I started to ignore him and set up camp, he must have figured he had dragged this out as long as he could and started to tell me what had happened.

When the chopper was trying to land on the side of the hill, the pilot could see there was no place to set down and told the door gunners, through the communication set, not to let either of us jump out. My side of the chopper had about a fifteen-foot fall, but the hill was so steep, the other side, Big John's side, had about a thirty-foot fall. When the door gunner grabbed my pack, it wasn't to push me out, as had been the rule in the past, but to tell me not to jump. At the same time the door gunner on the other side grabbed Big John's pack. Big John thought he was being thrown out, but he was so high up he grabbed onto the side of the door and hung on for dear life. Before the door gunner could talk to him, I had jumped, offsetting the balance of the whole chopper, which almost turned upside down. The pilot compensated and brought the chopper upright, after which it swung too far and the blade hit the hillside, almost causing the aircraft to crash in a ball of fire. I am sure the only thing that saved the chopper was the pilot's skill and experience.

Big John said when they got back to LZ Center and landed, the two pilots got out and were spitting mad. He said they checked the big overhead blade for damage and were cursing me the whole time. While Big John and the other team members sat there waiting, one of the door gunners told Big John the pilot wanted him to shoot at me with his machine gun as they passed my location. So what I thought was the helicopter coming back to see how I was, actually was the pilot in a blind fury, trying to get revenge on me for almost crashing his beloved aircraft. Big John told me he assured the door gunner he had done the right thing by not firing at me, even a warning shot. He told him I would not have just sat there, being shot at. I had a machine gun and would return fire, with deadly accuracy, probably killing everybody in the chopper. He told him I was crazy, and hated chopper pilots and their crews, and they were all lucky I didn't start shooting at them for leaving me. He said by the expression on the door gunner's face, the idea of me shooting back must not have occurred to him and he was sure the door gunner would relate this back to the pilot.

Big John and I started laughing. We both knew there was no way I was going to fire at a helicopter. I didn't hate chopper pilots and their crews; I envied them. When I asked Big John why he told them that, he said, "We can't let those flyboys think they can just toss us out the door whenever they want." He said, "I bet that door gunner has already told his pilot and the rest of that crew what I said and they will tell others. It's good for them to be afraid of us. Next time they will think twice before kicking some grunt out the door at twenty feet." Big John was a black man from some shit-hole in Detroit. He knew a thing or two about keeping face on the street. I learned a lot from him.

On the second evening, a chopper was scheduled to come out to our hill and bring us more water. It was amazing how much water four guys could drink just sitting around doing nothing. Out of boredom, I chose to meet the chopper and bring the water back. The command post back at center and I decided on a prearranged location where I would meet the chopper. I was sure the gooks knew where we were, on top of the hill, but we moved around after sunset to try to throw them off. I didn't see any reason to have the chopper land in our laps, showing anyone exactly where we were that night. I chose a spot as far away as possible, about a thousand yards away, and went to meet the chopper by myself. As I waited, it started to get dark and I became aware of being alone.

When I heard the chopper coming, I came out of the bushes and stood at one end of the clearing guiding the chopper down. My hands were raised over my head holding a sniper rifle with a large scope mounted on it that I had grabbed instead of my machine gun. The chopper wasn't going to land. It just barely touched down and dropped out two five-gallon jerry cans full of water. The LZ was small and, as always, the blast of wind from the chopper blade almost blew me over. I had to brace myself so I wouldn't fall down. I had forgotten to wear my shirt, the weather had been so hot, and the rocks and stuff being kicked up by the chopper pelted my bare chest and face and forced me to close my eyes. After the chopper rose up and started to leave, the wind died down and I opened my eyes.

To my complete amazement, there was a man standing next to the two water cans looking around, not quite sure what he should do next. He was a second lieutenant, dressed in brand new jungle fatigues, and looked completely out of place. I couldn't believe he was sent to us. Officers didn't go on OPs waiting to be slaughtered. This guy looked like he just got in-country. He had that clean look, and I realized he must have gotten off the chopper by mistake. That chopper must have been heading out to LZ Center from Chu Lai, and was just dropping off our water on the way. This guy, having never been to LZ Center, must have gotten off at the first stop the chopper made.

I could see this was going to be fun. He walked up to me and asked where the battalion command post was. I think he expected me to salute him. I silently thanked God for giving me this opportunity to play around with this green seed, uppity officer. I knew God doesn't grant us these gifts often, so I had to make the best of it. I pointed to LZ Center, answering his question truthfully. As he started to walk in that direction, he asked how far it was. I told him if he was going to walk there, he could probably make it in two days if he hurried. He walked back to me and said he had been told the battalion command post was on LZ Center. I told him it was, offering nothing more. I wasn't about to explain to this asshole what had happened.

I hated officers in general—it was my right as a grunt—but this guy wasn't even infantry. He was some communications officer sent out to LZ Center to sit on his ass in a bunker, giving guys like me a hard time when we got up on the hill. They always wanted us to salute them and told us to stay down on the bunker line; we didn't belong on top of the hill, where the water and food was. They told us that each bunker could send one man up for water once a day. Otherwise we were to stay on the bunker line and only come up for meals, one man from each bunker at a time.

He finally asked me if this was LZ Center. I told him no. He asked me where LZ Center was and I pointed again in the direction that I had before. He asked me what hill we were on now. I told him I didn't think it had a name; we were in the field. He asked me where my company was. I told him LZ Center. I could tell he was getting mad, but he looked at me closely for the first time. He started to see I had no clothes on except for pants and boots. I had on no helmet, rucksack, or pack of any kind. The only weapon I had was a sniper rifle with a huge scope. Even he could tell this was not standard issue. I told him it probably wasn't a good idea to stand there. We'd better grab the water and start moving before the gooks came; they probably heard the chopper and would be coming soon. That got his attention. He looked at me, letting that last comment pass, and again asked where my company was, where the other men were. I said, do you mean my company and my company commander and all its men? His face lit up and he said yes. I told him LZ Center was about a two-day hump from here and he'd better lower his voice and get moving. I said I would rather not be captured by the VC that night.

I started to move and he followed me. I motioned for him to stay low and he did. I grabbed the water cans and handed him one. He took it grudgingly and almost dropped it because of its weight—water is heavy. He followed me, half running, carrying the five-gallon can with both hands, trying not to make any noise while struggling with the awkward can. I stopped after about two hundred yards. The cans were heavy but I wasn't going to let him see that I thought so. When we stopped and I let him rest, I could see he was trying real hard to compose a question that I would answer, and from which he would receive usable information about his situation. He finally said, "Where are we going?" I told him back to our camp. He asked, "So there are other people with you? You aren't alone?" I brought my finger up to my lips to tell him to be quiet, and started walking again, fast. I was having more fun than any grunt should be allowed to have. Everything I said was true, but I didn't really think we were in any danger. I guess it's all your point of view. We were in Vietnam; we were on a jungle hilltop with VC all around. I didn't think any of them were within a couple of miles. I didn't think the VC were coming up to kill us, but I suppose they might be. It was dark now, and the lieutenant couldn't see my face when I smiled.

The rest of my team wouldn't expect me back yet, even in the dark. They had heard the chopper, so they knew when I got the water. They knew how heavy two five-gallon jerrycans of water were, and how I would carry one in each hand with the rifle on my back in its leather sling. That's why I brought the sniper rifle in the first place, because of the sling. Nobody kept a sling on an M-16 in a rifle company. It would take too long to get it off your back when something happened, and you wanted to keep your hands ready. The team knew I would walk a short way and stop and rest, then walk another short way and rest. There was no hurry. When I say the team I mean Big John; the other two were green seeds and their opinion didn't matter. Big John was going to like the gift I was bringing him. I was hoping it would make up for me almost killing him with that chopper thing the day before.

At our next rest stop the lieutenant asked his question again and I was ready for him. He asked again if there were other people with me or if I was alone. I had him whisper it real quiet in my ear, motioning to him there could be others around who might hear him if he was too loud. I answered very slowly, almost touching his ear with my lips, "No, I am not alone. You are with me." I picked up my water can and rifle and moved off quickly. I had to or I would have fallen on the ground laughing. This guy must have thought I was some lone sniper who had gone insane, living out in the jungle for months at a time. He didn't know I was joking, and he was getting scared. At the next stop he asked if there would be anybody else at my camp besides us, and if there were any people there now. I told him yes, there were other men there. I could hear his sigh of relief. Now he knew he had really screwed up, but at least he wasn't out here alone with this nut. He asked, "About how many of you are there?" I said, "Including you and me, five."

I told him to stay put. I was going to go into the camp; it wasn't far and I would come back and get him shortly. I told him if something happened to stay in the area but get off the main trail we were on. I couldn't see his face but I could tell he didn't want me to leave. He had no idea we were on a trail, or why he would want to get off it. I was not joking about me going into camp alone. Big John was only expecting one man coming back. If he heard two, he might start shooting. I came into camp with our signal and Big John told me he already knew what was going on. The hill had been on the horn telling us it was too dark to take the second lieutenant out tonight, and to keep him safe until a chopper was sent for him in the morning. This reminded me of when I got off the dust-off at the wrong hospital, and how nicely I was treated by my officers when I returned. I went back and got our royal guest.

I sat him down, explained where we were, and what our mission was according to the hill. I thought this was an excellent time to explain my tethered-goat theory, and how I thought we were just there to be slaughtered, so the hill could have advance notice of an all-out attack. He could see there were in fact only five of us, including him, and he didn't even have a gun. We all took turns telling him war stories. I don't think he slept one minute all night. Big John caught on quickly and he would startle everybody by saying, "What's that? I thought I heard something!" or "I got movement on the flank! " real loud. We would all act like something was happening, grabbing our weapons and hunkering down like we were waiting to be overrun by the NVA hordes. Big John pointed out to the lieutenant that since he was an officer, the VC would probably not kill him outright, like us. They would probably take him back to a secure area and interrogate him. We all gave him helpful hints on how to kill himself if the pain got too bad.

The next morning I walked him back to the same LZ where I had found him the night before. He didn't have the same clean look that he had when he first got off that chopper, only ten hours before. This was one hill rat, second Louie who was going to think twice before he cussed out some grungy grunt for hanging out trying to get some extra food, or some cigarettes. It seemed all the good cigarettes like Marlborough and Lucky Strikes stayed on the hill and only the shit cigarettes, like Kent and Cool, got out to the field. I thanked him for dropping in, telling him it was too bad he couldn't stay longer. He smiled sheepishly and declined, saying, "I think I will pass on that invitation." I guided the chopper in, he got on, the chopper took off, and I never saw him again.

"In Heaven there is no beer
That's why we drink it here
And when we're all gone from here
Our friends will be drinking all the beer"

BEER RUN

One day, out of the blue, we got orders to go to LZ Ross. We were told a typhoon was coming and all ground forces were ordered out of the field and assigned to fire support bases until the typhoon passed. One minute we were trudging through the jungle, and the next minute we were told to cut a landing zone, and choppers came in and whisked us away to LZ Ross.

To us, LZ Ross was the land of milk and honey. It had hot chow for each meal and unlimited supplies of C-rations to eat between the hot meals. We had good water to drink all the time and cold milk with each meal. All this was nice, but the most incredible item they had was a bar, a real bar that sold cold beer. Some entrepreneur in an artillery unit had turned an underground bunker into a bar, and our company was allowed to buy beer there.

All we had to do in exchange for all this was pull perimeter duty at night. Each position had a bunker built of sandbags and a steel framework. Our platoon was assigned to bunkers on the side of the firebase that was facing a village. A swamp was between our assigned bunkers and the village about three hundred yards away. The permanent personnel assigned to the firebase must have thought they were pulling a fast one by assigning us these bunkers. It seems the local VC would come into the village each night and shoot a few rounds into the closest bunkers, ours, just to let the GIs know they were still out there. We would have done just about anything to live like this all the time.

The bar thing didn't last long. My squad got to drink some beer on the first day, but after we left one of our other platoons went in and got drunk. I guess some guys shot up the place—I never got the whole story—and our entire company was forbidden to go near the bar. We were told this restriction would remain in effect until we left the firebase in four or five days. The base commander told our company commander something like, "If your men can't act like normal human beings, we will treat them like animals." We weren't like normal human beings—we lived in the jungle and killed people. We hadn't had any replacements in months, so the only men left in our company were the strongest and the fastest. The weaker and slower ones were in body bags. They didn't need the beer; we did.

On our third day there, our squad was assigned a mission to provide security for a minesweeping unit. There was a road about a quarter mile long that ran from the firebase to the main highway that had to be swept for land mines each morning. All the roads that I saw in Vietnam were dirt. I guess the local VC liked to mine this road in addition to shooting at the bunkers closest to the village.

The unit consisted of two minesweepers and a huge dump truck called the "Abortion." Someone had painted the name on the side of the truck in white paint. The two minesweepers would walk out in front of the truck with metal detectors, swinging them back and forth. They were also looking for fresh dirt. The truck would drive down the road, about two hundred feet behind the men sweeping with the metal detectors. If the sweepers missed any land mines, the weight of the truck would set them off. The dump truck was full of dirt, to give it more weight, and it had been redesigned to be driven backward. The cab had been refitted so the driver could perch on top of it, facing the back of the truck. The steering wheel, the clutch and gear shift, and the brake were all refitted to work on the driver's perch. There was armor around the driver for protection from snipers, but the top was open in case the truck hit a mine; ideally, the force of the explosion would push the driver up and out. The driver was already twelve feet off the ground; if he was blown out the top of the perch by the force of an exploding mine he was going to need a parachute to get down safely. The truck was a very odd-looking piece of equipment. I guess that's how it got its name.

The minesweepers and the truck driver were rewarded for doing this dangerous job by getting the rest of the day off. I found out the truck driver stayed high on pot all day and was probably whacked out when he drove the truck in the morning. His superiors knew what he was doing, but if they busted him, who else could they find stupid enough to drive a truck over a potential minefield everyday? As security for the minesweeping team, my machine gun squad walked behind the truck—far behind the truck. We were there in case some snipers opened up on the minesweepers. It was easy duty. Nothing ever happened, and at the end of the road we got to go into the small village.

There wasn't much in the village, but there were young girls in pretty dresses. The first thing the girls did when we got into the village was to come up to each one of us and put what they called love beads around ours necks and ask us if we had girlfriends. When we said we didn't, they would ask us if they could be our girlfriends. It seems we had a different definition of the word "girlfriend" than they had. Our interpretation of this type of girlfriend was let's go have sex, now. Their definition was for us to give them money, jewelry or anything else, then they'd smile at us and meet us again the next day, after the mine sweep, to take more money or anything else we would give them.

This was going nowhere fast and we were about to leave to go back to the fire support base when one of the girls asked if we wanted to buy beer. These were magic words. When the firebase commander restricted us from buying beer at the bar, he also forbid our company to have any alcohol at all—something about not wanting his personnel killed by these insubordinate troops. We said yes, we did want to buy beer, but how could we get it back on the fire support base? The MPs at the front gate were not going to let us back in with beer; the whole fire support base knew about us by now. That's when the girls told us how it was done. We would place our order now—beer, liquor, pot, whatever we wanted—and agree upon a price. Then one of us would come at sundown with the money and meet one of the girls at no man's land. We would exchange the money for the booze and come back to our bunker and have a party. No man's land was the swamp in front of our bunker—the bunker nobody else wanted because they all thought it was so dangerous—the closest point from the fire support base to the village.

We had been told the swamp was ringed by razor wire and trip flares, and the Viet Cong could never infiltrate through there. I guess nobody told the girls this, because it sounded like they did it all the time. The girls even told us which bunker to meet them in front of—Bunker 39, our bunker—and where there was a blue ribbon tied to one of the steel stakes holding up the razor wire. The stake with the blue ribbon was right where they said it was, about five hundred feet out from our bunker. We made our deal with the girls for an order of beer and whiskey and pot. It was a small order; we weren't sure it wasn't just a trick to expose ourselves and get shot by the VC. I suppose the girls didn't trust us either.

Sundown came and we had to decide who was going to crawl out there on his belly, very slowly, through a snake-infested swamp, razor wire, trip flares, and who knows what else, to what could be a Viet Cong ambush. After all, the village was taken over by the Viet Cong each night. That's where the incoming rounds came from, that village. There was no question who would go—The Man. His name was Tommy Manford, and he loved beer more than life itself; he jumped at this chance to prove it. The Man was from Chicago, and was the nicest guy you would ever want to meet—not real smart, but honest and trustworthy. He was not going there to impress anyone, he was just afraid someone else would screw it up and maybe chicken out at the last minute and not bring back the beer. Usually he said very little, but this day his comment was something like, "I'm not trusting any of you assholes to fuck this up. I'm going out there, and if I have to deal with the VC themselves, I'm coming back with the beer." When it came to acquiring beer, nobody argued with The Man.

Although we were the same age as college kids, we were not college kids. This was no fraternity prank. We wanted a drug-induced escape from the daily horrors we faced. The security of being on this fire support base would allow us to get drunk and make noise, something we could never do in the bush. It was something we desperately wanted. Desperate people do desperate things. Unlike the rest of the hundreds of men on this base, we were going back to the jungle in a few days. We knew some of us would be coming out in body bags. Because the base commander refused to let us have any alcohol, we did what was necessary. This was our only chance to have a little fun. If The Man had thought we could get beer by throwing a grenade into the base commander's bunker and killing him, he would have done it. Our concern for his safety and well-being was about as much as his concern for ours. For this reason, the base commander kept two armed guards at his bunker door twenty-four hours a day; they weren't just for the VC.

Sundown came and The Man went out to get the beer. We had my machine gun set up on top of our bunker and we borrowed another machine gun and set it up on the next bunker down. This gave us a crossfire of M-60 firepower. We got hold of a starlight scope, the first generation of night vision technology, and set it up on a tripod with a man acting as a spotter right next to my machine gun. This way, he could direct my fire if it got too dark. Another spotter with a powerful set of binoculars was on the other side, close to my ear to call out targets. If this was an ambush, the Viet Cong would be sorry. They may think they were dealing with a bunch of goof-offs from the fire support base, but this is what we did for a living every day.

A machine gun doesn't work like a rifle. You don't just aim at the target and pull the trigger; you aim in the general direction of the target and fire a five-round burst. Every fifth round was a tracer round; the tip of the bullet was painted with red magnesium. The magnesium would burn very brightly as the bullet traveled. It burned brightly enough to be seen in broad sunlight, which allowed the machine gunner to see exactly where his rounds were hitting. The reason for the burst of five rounds at once was to let the gun jump around so all the bullets would not land in the same place. This created a sort of rain of bullets landing, like holding a hose to water your lawn. The water starts out at the same point, but spreads out over a distance and comes down in small droplets like rain. That's how a machine gun works if handled properly. It creates what is known as a "killing zone," a rain of bullets that is hard for your targets to escape from once you are zeroed in on them.

This was the perfect terrain for this type of weapon. I was an expert with the M-60 machine gun—I'd had a lot of practice—and with two spotters to control the fire and a second machine gun to expand the killing zone, we were ready. We also had four men with M-79 grenade launchers and they had an unlimited supply of rounds, something we never had in the field. The rest of the men were armed with M-16s, each man with five bandoleers of loaded clips. If sniper fire came from the village, our "girlfriends" were going to get a hot date that night.

We had strict orders, given by the base commander, not to fire into the village without first calling in to command and getting specific permission to fire. In our world, if someone shot at you, you shot back. We could not have cared less what that guy said; if sniper rounds were fired at The Man coming from the village, we were going to light it up. Tracer rounds fired at thatched roofs would set the roofs on fire. If we took in sniper rounds from that village while The Man was out there, we would burn the village down. Manford went out at sunset, met the girl with the booze, paid her, and came back in—no ambush, no problems. A good time was had by all. After The Man got back and we all started drinking in the bunker, we did get sniper fire. But we were all safe inside the bunker, getting a good buzz on, and nobody cared. The thing that did bother us was that while we were drinking, The Man said the girl he met out in no man's land with the booze wasn't one of the young girls in the pretty dresses that we met in the village that morning. He said this one was older, was in black pajamas, and looked like a VC.

The next morning we volunteered for the security patrol again and when we got to the village the same young girls in pretty dresses were there with their smiles. We placed our order for booze for that night, but because we had had to use another machine gun for security the night before, we had to tell the other gun squad what was going on and they wanted to get in on the "beer run," as it was now being called. Our order for booze this time was much bigger; it was going to take two girls to bring it out and a helper for Manford to bring it in. The girls were very happy to take our order; they must have worked on commission. During our negotiation over prices, we brought up the subject of sniper fire and the fact that we were worried about them setting us up for an ambush. At that point the smiles went away. The girl who seemed to be in charge told us there would be nothing to worry about as long as they got their money. We would have thirty minutes after the exchange before the sniper fire would start.

So there it was—we were doing business with the Viet Cong. Surprisingly, I don't remember anybody having a problem with that. I have to admit we had discussed having The Man meet the girl and taking the booze without paying them. Based on this new information, seeing we were doing business with the Viet Cong and not a bunch of bimbos, it made good sense to pay them, as per the original plan. That sundown things were much more relaxed. The fix was in and we had our own little cease-fire agreement. We still had our defenses ready, but we didn't expect any trouble. It was a simple business deal; we paid them money for the goods we wanted.

This was still combat, and in combat anything could happen; you just didn't know what. The ambush came, but not from the direction we expected. The enemy hit us from the rear. As The Man was out in no man's land making the exchange, I was up on top of our bunker, manning the machine gun with my spotters. One of the spotters tapped my shoulder to get my attention, and pointed to a man walking down the perimeter road coming toward our bunker. We had been focusing so much on looking for the gooks to ambush us, we didn't even think of watching the road behind us, coming from inside the fire support base.

This captain walked up the road behind our bunker, holding an M-79 grenade launcher. He stopped behind the bunker, staying on the road, and fired three rounds at the location of the exchange, the steel stake with the blue ribbon tied to it. An M-79 grenade launcher is a single-shot weapon. It's like a short single-shot shotgun, but with a much wider barrel, 44 millimeters.

It can fire a variety of rounds: high explosives, which explode like a hand grenade when they hit the ground; beehive rounds, which are a lot of small lead balls like bird shot from a shotgun; and CS rounds, which release CS gas when the rounds land on the ground. CS gas is a sort of tear gas; we all had to endure the gas chamber in basic training where they showed you firsthand the effects of this brutal gas. This is what the captain fired at the steel stake where the exchange was going on. He fired the first shot and waited for it to land. It was too far, so he adjusted and fired the second and third shot. We were dumbfounded. We didn't know what to do, so we did nothing. The captain just turned away after firing and walked away smiling; he thought this was a game.

The Man and his helper came back with the booze. He was gasping for air and his eyes were red from the effects of the gas, but The Man wasn't about to let a little thing like not being able to breathe stop him from carrying out the beer and other packages.

That night while we were drinking our spoils, we discussed the problem of the captain who had fired the M-79. If he had come down and said, "Look you guys, we know what you are doing and if we catch you doing it again, we are sending down a squad of MPs and arresting everyone at this bunker and sending you all to LBJ," that probably would have been the end of it. But he didn't. This REMF came down by himself and fired on one of our own men. And this captain wasn't even infantry; he was wearing an artillery insignia. Had one of our own officers come down and told us to knock it off, that would be it, no questions asked. We obeyed orders from our own, to the letter, no discussions. But we hadn't seen one of our own officers or platoon sergeants in days. They were probably cooped up in a bunker doing the same thing we were—getting as drunk as possible to brace up for going back to the field. Instead, this "entitled" captain took it upon himself to come down to our neck of the perimeter and try to deny us what little pleasure we might have, and then smile about it. So it was agreed—if he came back the next night, our last night there, we would kill him.

There were two Johns in our bunker. There was Big John, a big black guy from Detroit, and John from New York City. He was from one of the "B"s—Brooklyn or the Bronx—I forget which one. John had spent a good part of his youth in jail and at his last sentencing, for armed robbery, the judge gave him an option. He told me the judge said, "If you like waving a gun around and threatening people, maybe you should go to Vietnam and see how you like it there." John agreed and here he was. John agreed to take care of the captain if he was stupid enough to come back the next night. Done right, the captain's death would be seen as a result of sniper fire. This was a war zone. From our point of view, the captain had nothing but contempt for grunts. He was doing this out of spite. "See, I am an officer. I can do anything I want to you low-life grunts, and I am going to stop you from getting this booze even if your own officers won't." He had probably gone to our company commander and told him what was going on, and knowing our CO, he probably laughed at him. To us, killing him was all right; he was choosing to stick his nose into something that did not involve him.

He had the choice, on the other hand, trying to kill the Viet Cong who were selling us the beer, whiskey and pot, now that would be flat-out wrong. The local Viet Cong were conducting an honest business deal. They were stuck in this war, too. They were only trying to make a few bucks on the side. The North Vietnamese government and the United States had their cease-fire; we were having one of our own. If anyone was stupid enough to get in the way, for a lark, he should be prepared for the consequences. We were. We knew if we got caught killing one of our officers we would all go to jail for a long time, but the chances of getting caught were small. Besides, if you went to jail at least you got out of the field. John carried an M-14 retooled for accuracy, with a sniper scope.

Sundown came and The Man was ready to go out and get the biggest load yet. Word had spread to the other bunkers, and everybody wanted in on the beer run. We had ordered four cases of beer, two quarts of whiskey, and about five decks of joints. A deck of joints was ten marijuana cigarettes in a plastic bag; each joint was about the size of a Cuban cigar. The beers cost us one dollar each, so that was twenty-four dollars for a case. A beer cost ten cents in a Chu-Lai enlisted man's bar and twenty-five cents at the fire support bar where we were banned, but on the black market it cost a buck. Whisky cost about twenty-five dollars a quart. The deck of joints cost one dollar per deck. That's right; a beer was a dollar but a joint the size of a big cigar, which could get a whole squad high, cost ten cents each. Supply and demand. That meant The Man was going out there to no man's land with one hundred fifty-one dollars of our money. A grunt got paid about one hundred ninety dollars per month, including combat pay. To us, this was almost a month's pay; it was a lot of money.

The Man started crawling out to meet the VC to get our order. He had a helper for the heavy load and a .45-caliber pistol in the small of his back, just in case. We had the road covered in both directions. We had lookouts farther down the road with PRC-25 radios to warn us if a tank or anything else was coming down the road. Who knew what the captain was going to do this time? Whatever is was, we were ready if he came. He would not be laughing when it was over.

We watched The Man crawl out the five hundred feet to make the exchange. Our expectations were high and we were all very tense. Out of nowhere, a chopper dropped in right over The Man and opened fire with its side rockets. The entire swamp was filled with a cloud of CS gas in seconds. The Man came stumbling back, without the prize, gagging and spitting up. He was much worse than the night before; there was a lot more gas. Just to add a little salt to our wound, a breeze brought the cloud of gas past our bunker. All we could do was sit there with our eyes burning until the cloud dispersed and moved on. After the gas stopped burning and it got dark, The Man and I went back out to the steel stake with the blue ribbon. The Man said he had seen the girls coming with our order. After the gas hit, he was sure he saw them drop the beer and stuff and run off. We went back out and tried to find it. There was nothing; they must have doubled back and got the stuff. I didn't think the Viet Cong waiting in the village would be too happy if the girls came back without the beer or the money.

I can still remember sitting on the bunker watching the chopper drop in and fire its rockets. I remember looking at the turbine and the heat and flame shooting out the back. I worked for Pratt and Whitney Jet Engines in East Hartford, Connecticut, before I was drafted. I worked assembling jet engines and knew how the blades turned inside a jet engine. That's all these turbines were, small jet engines. The tolerance between the turning rings of blades was only a few thousandths of an inch. As soon as I realized what was going on, what the chopper was doing, I couldn't help but think what a few five-round bursts would do to the turbine powering that helicopter. It took every bit of control I had not to shoot it down. It was only about fifty feet off the ground and hovering in a steady position. From my position on the bunker, I couldn't have missed.

We sat around the rest of the night cussing out the captain. Nobody saw him in the chopper, but we were all sure he was there. We would have been crying in our beer if we had any. He had won; he beat us. The stupid grunts will now learn not to fool with him the next time we come to his base. We all agreed we should have just killed him that first night, and next time we would.

The next morning our company mounted choppers and went back into the bush. Instead of hangovers we just had regrets. That night I was out on ambush. It was raining and I was sitting behind my machine gun on some jungle path ready to kill anyone coming down the trail. I kept seeing the face of that captain laughing as he fired the M-79 that first night. I kept imagining he was laughing as he was telling the story to his friends, in their officers' club.

FUNNY MONEY

MPC, or Military Payment Currency, is what we used as money in Vietnam. We used to call it Monopoly money because it was made out of brightly colored paper and looked like the play money used in Monopoly. Only military personnel were supposed to have it.

All the Vietnamese people used it; it was the standard currency used for everyday trade. Even the Viet Cong used MPC. It was against the law for United States military personnel to be in possession of an American greenback. You were better off being caught with pot than with a twenty-dollar bill American. The official money of South Vietnam was called dong; nobody used it.

One night about midnight, a secret operation took place throughout the entire country of South Vietnam. Every finance office in the country was segmented off with a special unit of security. Then key finance officers entered the finance offices with cases of new MPC. Their job was to collect all the old MPC and replace it with new MPC. The new MPC was made of different colored paper, so if a one-dollar bill MPC was yellow, then the new one-dollar bill might be green. An old ten-dollar bill MPC could have been blue and the new ten-dollar bill would be red. This was all coordinated to happen at the same time throughout the whole country. The reason for the change was to try to stop, or at least slow down, the black market.

The black market is where civilian Vietnamese would get a hold of goods that were brought into Vietnam by the US military. They got this stuff—beer, liquor, cigarettes, guns—by hook or by crook and sold it to any willing buyer, at whatever price the market would bear. To me it sounded like good old capitalism but the military didn't see it that way.

The net result of this operation was that in a twenty-four hour period all the old MPC was worthless. All the money that the street merchants, hookers, drug dealers, or anybody else had saved from their business dealings was lost. If you were in the US military you could change it over to the new MPC. This was a big deal; fortunes were made and lost by this change, all within one day. See, if you were military you could go up to a gook who had some old MPC and tell him you would change it to new MPC, but it was going to cost him fifty percent—two old for one new. Enlisted men could only change over a limited amount, around two hundred dollars, but officers could change over all they wanted. That way enlisted guys only got to steal a little, while the officers got to steal as much as they could get their hands on, within the twenty-four hour period. I heard stories of some officers making tens of thousands of dollars by changing the old MPC of madams of large whorehouses—RHIP (rank has its privileges). That's the macro side of this economic up-heaval; us grunts were only concerned about the micro side.

As a general rule, money didn't play a very important part of a grunt's life. But as always, having a little pocket change was nice, even in the jungle. You needed money to gamble with, buy the other guy's canned peaches, or buy that envied food the canned pound cake, the most valuable item in a case of C-rations. Some-body was always going on R&R or going home and it was nice to have some money to buy that pack of Marlboro cigarettes that he didn't need anymore; cigarettes in the Cs were usually crap.

There were also the times you went into a village out in the middle of nowhere and some old mama san would come up to you with black, beetle nut–stained teeth and hold out a can of Coke saying, "One dollar." I could never figure out where they got the Coke. When that happened, it was nice to have a dollar in your pocket to buy the Coke. Another reason to have money was in case you got hit and dusted off to a hospital; that instantly put you back in a world where money mattered. Of course, if you went into the hospital unconscious, chances were some orderly would steal your money before you woke up.

So, while it seemed like every REMF in the country was making a fortune off the backs of these hookers (no pun intended) by changing their old MPC, we were out in the field making another kind of killing. I remember coming back from a patrol one day, hot, sweaty and tired as always and the lieutenant came over to us and asked us if we had any money. Now that was an odd question. He explained the whole MPC change thing and he also mentioned that while we were out on a four-hour patrol, humping through the jungle, a finance officer came out from Chu Lai and changed everybody's MPC. If we had any money we missed the boat and what we had was now worthless.

This was not good. We happened to be bivouacked near my favorite refugee camp and were going to be there for the next couple of days. This meant we actually had a place to buy stuff. It's not like there was a store there but they did have beer and soda, "one dollar." Of course, we were on that patrol and missed the MPC change and our money was worthless.

This is the type of thing I just won't take. I already had money issues with the Army and this pushed me over the top. When I first got to the company and was filling out forms I was asked if I wanted to send an allotment home—that means they would take a certain amount of my pay each month and send it home. I agreed and had most of the money sent home keeping about twenty dollars for myself. You didn't need a lot of money; it was just nice to have a few bucks stashed away in your rucksack just in case. We had been warned it would be stupid to get your whole paycheck in the field because you would lose it. It's just plain paper and it rots in hot humid weather.

Also, if you keep a large amount of money in your pocket you are likely to lose it during a clothing exchange. You didn't get to keep your own clothes; a laundry sergeant would come out with a re-supply ship every week or so with a bunch of duffel bags of washed fatigues. You would strip down, throw your dirty rotten fatigues in a pile, and then fight naked with everybody else over the clean fatigues as they were emptied out of the duffel bags onto the ground. I am a big guy and it was hard to get stuff that fit. I don't mean that looked good, just pants that I could get on and not split. No one wore underwear; it just wasn't practical. You emptied your pockets of everything that had value, but money could easily get left behind. You were mostly looking for knives or heat tabs, something that had weight to it. Money was something that you didn't think of until you needed it and I am sure I threw away a lot of money with the dirty fatigues.

I shouldn't have had much money with me anyway because I was only supposed to get twenty dollars for pay, per month, but a mistake was made and they brought my whole pay amount out each month and I had all that MPC to try to hold on to, on top of everything else. I tried to explain my situation to the payroll officer each month when he came out to the field to pay us but he wouldn't look up at me. I just was told to "move along." I had no place to hold on to it and I misplaced most of it. After about six months in country I got in line to get my pay one day and the payroll officer snapped his head up and looked at me after I told him my name. He said, "So, you are Boyd. You are the one that has been conspiring to cheat the United States government out of $198 each month. Well, I found out about your plan and put a stop to it." It seems my allotment was going home after all and they had been paying me double for six months.

That's when he told me I wouldn't be getting any more pay for the next six months. He added I was lucky he wasn't going to bring me up on charges. He screws up my pay records and says he's letting me off the hook. There was nothing I could do. I could have shot him but I thought better of it. I was planning to go on R&R and I was holding out as long as I could, trying not to go too soon so I would have something to look forward to. I noticed sometimes guys that went on R&R that were short (little time left in country), never came back to the field. They sometimes got jobs in the rear or on LZ Center. That was my fantasy, going on R&R and coming back and getting a job in the rear like the laundry guy, coming out once in a while with the re-supply ship and going back with the dirty laundry. Well, that was my fantasy when I wasn't fantasizing about women. Of course, in the job-in-the-rear fantasy there were women from the village in Chu Lai, so I guess it was all the same fantasy.

The fantasy was no good now because you couldn't go on R&R if you didn't have at least two hundred dollars on you. They wanted to see the money at the R&R center in Da Nang—no money, no R&R. I guess the military didn't want guys roaming around foreign countries begging for money. So now I had a big problem. I had to get two hundred dollars before I could even think of going on R&R and getting that job in the rear. I figured on holding out for another three months before requesting my R&R. This wouldn't make me very short when I got back, but it was the best I could do. All that was on my mind when this MPC change came up, and what little money I had, was suddenly no good. I had to start from scratch.

That was all in the future. Right now, coming back from that patrol and finding out my money was worthless, I had to do something about my current situation—no money for Coke. Once I realized what had happened, I figured the only way I could get any value out of my old MPC was to fool the local villagers by changing all my old MPC into goods, coke, beer, pot, whatever, then I could sell whatever I didn't want to other GIs for the new MPC. But I had to move fast; I figured the word would get around fast.

I tried to buy some stuff at the usual places but all I got was dirty looks. One guy I knew, a PF (Popular Forces), took me into the back room of his hooch and showed me a cigar box full of old MPC. He begged me to help him change the old money for him but I couldn't. I left him with his head hanging, a defeated man with a wife and three kids to support. I liked this guy. We had been on a number of patrols together and I once saved his life by killing a water buffalo that was charging him and was going to trample him—microeconomics.

I could see I was too late. News about the MPC change had been spreading like wildfire and these people were good businessmen; I was no match for them. My only hope was to go much farther out to some of the small hooch areas that had sprung up near the refugee camp like gold towns in the old West. Perhaps they hadn't heard yet, I might still have a chance. I borrowed an M-16 and some clips, emptied out my rucksack for the goods, and headed off to the outer realms of gook land, VC territory.

I went out as far as I dared alone. It was only money and I didn't want to die for it. I found a few poor dumb bastards who hadn't got the word yet and bought all their stuff, a few cans of soda and beer. They were poor, they had been uprooted from their homes in the first place or they wouldn't have been there, probably spent their last few dong on some black market stuff they had heard they could make a few bucks on by selling to the GIs and because they were so far out from the safety of the PF security forces they probably had to deal with the VC at night coming into their houses and taking what they wanted and terrorizing them with threats about what would happen to them if they were found fraternizing with the Americans. So these poor bastards risked their lives selling a few cans of soda and beer to a GI and I ripped them off with the old MPC. I felt so proud.

A day or two later I found myself in Chu Lai and I bumped into J.J. again at our company's rear area. He was my assistant gunner when he wasn't in the hospital from getting shot. He was coming from the hospital again from another wound. I was only going to be in Chu Lai one day and was going back to the company the next day so I wanted to go to a bar that night and drink beer until I fell down. I had drunk the few beers and sodas that I had stolen from the refugees, and my MPC was no good so I had thrown it away. A cold beer at the enlisted man's club in Chu Lai was ten cents, but it might as well have been ten dollars if you didn't have any money—microeconomics. I asked J.J. if he had any money. He said he did but it was the old MPC; he had been asleep in his hospital bed when the finance officer had come around to make the change and no one woke him up.

Only J.J. would hold on to that worthless paper. He held it up to show me like it meant something. He only had two ten-dollar bills old MPC, but looking at him holding it there gave me an idea. I asked him if I could change his old worthless MPC for new MPC if I could I have half. He readily agreed but said, "How you gunna do that?" in his slow Southern drawl. I didn't bother to answer, I just got up and grabbed the two tens and took off. I told him to wait there; I would be back. I didn't want him coming with me, with his Bible Belt morality, on a mission of larceny.

I knew just what to do. I headed for the Chu Lai Orientation Center. If I could steal the food from the mouths of poor refugees, I could sure run a scam on some new green seeds just into the country a few days. I didn't want J.J. there to screw things up with a fit of honesty.

My idea was to go to the Orientation Center, where everybody comes when they first enter the country. I would go into their barracks and start talking to some guys, tell them a few war stories and ingratiate myself with them. Then, when I had their trust, I was going to ask them if anyone could break a ten-dollar MPC bill. These guys were brand new; they couldn't tell old MPC from new MPC and would give me change in new MPC for the old worthless MPC. It worked perfectly. I had to do it twice because I had to change the two ten-dollar bills and it didn't make sense to ask the same group of guys twice. Looking back I think those guys got a fair exchange for their money. I gave them good advice on what to expect when they got to their line company's permanent point and stuff like that, things to expect that none of the undead in their new squads would tell them because the undead didn't talk to green seeds. Fair exchange or not, I got their money and went back to get J.J.

We went to the EM Club and drank ten-cent beers until they closed the place and threw us out. Microeconomics.

REST & RECREATION

My orders finally came through for an R&R (Rest & Recreation) that I had requested months before. Everybody is entitled to one R&R, although the personnel in the rear seemed to get their one R&R four or five times during their one-year tour of duty. I was going to Australia. The day came for me to go into Chu Lai from the field and go to Da Nang the next day to catch a plane to Australia. I always wanted to go to Australia and this was sure a good time to get out of the field, because things were heating up with enemy activity.

My problem was my platoon was going out on patrol, and I was afraid if I went with them I wouldn't get back in time to get a chopper back to LZ Center and then Chu Lai. My lieutenant disagreed. He said he needed every man out there. Things were hairy, and I was the most qualified with the M-60 and I was going.

As we were talking, the battalion commander's chopper landed at our lager site. The sergeant major, top NCO of the entire battalion, got out and our company commander got in the colonel's chopper and they took off for an aerial inspection of the "situation." I saw my chance and took it. I broke the biggest rule of military protocol: I broke the chain of command. I went up to the sergeant major, pleaded my case, and produced my orders. Being old school, he said orders are orders. He told me to sit down on that spot and don't move until the colonel's chopper returns, get on the chopper, and carry out your orders. Of course, the lieutenant actually outranked the sergeant major, but no second lieutenant in his right mind would go up against a sergeant major, so I stayed. Someone else took my machine gun and off they went on their patrol. I have no idea where that colonel and our captain went with his chopper, but for three hours I sat there straining to hear that *woop-woop-woop* sound a chopper makes. I didn't get up, lie down, or even lean back for the whole three hours. I was afraid the sergeant major would see me move and take back his promise of taking me on that chopper with him.

The patrol came back before the chopper came. The guy who took my machine gun got killed and some other guy got hit and dusted off. They all seemed to be looking at me in disgust as they filed past, because I got out of the patrol by saying I was going to miss my chopper. Finally, the chopper came and I got back to Chu Lai. I went to the CP room and asked the clerk for my R&R orders to Australia. He told me some lieutenant had just taken my orders to Australia, which were hard to get, and left me some tickets to Hong Kong. He pointed out the lieutenant walking away from us and I ran out to confront him. After a brief conversation the lieutenant, who worked there in the rear and had never been out to the field, informed me that I was not going to Australia, he was. If I didn't want to go to Hong Kong for my R&R he would be happy to cut me some orders to send me back to the field the next morning. I went to Hong Kong.

THE TOOTH FAIRY

When I got back from my R&R in Hong Kong I expected to spend a few days in the rear relaxing before the top sergeant kicked me out of our rear area and made me go back out to the field. Even though that was the way it had been done in the past we had a new first sergeant now and this guy wasn't having any part of that. This was the new first sergeant's third tour in Vietnam and he was a prick.

The next morning everybody in the rear holding area was woken up early and brought out to a chopper pad to go back out to the field. The new first sergeant prick was there personally to make sure there were no shammers. In my book, it was a grunt's right to sham after R&R; you needed that in-between time to go from a hotel room in Hong Kong, with wall-to-wall women and booze, to life back in a line company in Vietnam. It was called being in R&R love. I am not sure if that name refers to the women or just the whole R&R experience, but the name sure fit.

So that morning the new first sergeant prick got us rounded up and personally came with us in the truck and waited with us at the chopper pad in Chu Lai. A Chinook was to take us to LZ Center where we could catch the next chopper going out to Black Death. He wanted to be sure we got on and didn't get lost. I thought, how nice of him.

A big Chinook came in and landed just long enough for us to board and then took off. We couldn't sit down because it was so loaded with supplies; it was the morning milk run. It was carrying other supplies as well, but it was actually loaded down with cartons of fresh cold milk like we had in school. The Chinook went from fire base to fire base, off-loading milk and other supplies at each stop. Then it would rise up and kind of slant forward until you could feel the power of its turbines pulling the huge aircraft through the air. Every time we took off I thought, here it comes; the next place we land will be LZ Center and I will be back. Not all the way back, but back far enough to smell the stench of the jungle and death. I wanted that hotel room in Hong Kong; that's the smell I wanted—R&R love. The chopper settled down and I looked outside to see where we were. It wasn't LZ Center; it was LZ Ross. That was it. I was getting off.

Another guy had gotten off the chopper with me. His name was Jack. He was from a different platoon and I didn't know him well. I had heard him talking about Australia; he had just gotten back from R&R. I could see he had a case of R&R love, too. We started talking and he agreed we had gotten a fast shuffle when that new first sergeant prick kicked us out of Chu Lai so fast. He had seen me getting off the Chinook and he didn't want to be left behind.

There was a wooden picnic table there and it was as good a place as any to hang out. Jack had a case of orange soda that he was bringing back to his squad. We started drinking the soda and talked all morning.

Jack was from New York City and worked for a while as a longshoreman, but he was a real sharp guy and soon got a job with the magazine *Sports Illustrated*. He said he had worked in the mailroom, reading the mail. He was one of a group of young guys who were paid to read the mail sent to the magazine, then sort out the bad letters or common letters and cull out the good ones and send them upstairs to the next level for possible publication. He tried to engage me in sports talk but it was no use; I have no interest in sports. We found plenty of stuff to talk about, but the most important thing we had in common was that we had decided to take a stand. We were not going back to the field, at least not that day.

The conversation got slow around noon. We didn't say anything to each other but I could tell we were both starting to get worried about what was going to happen to us, being AWOL and all. The Spec-4 who ran the chopper pad had entered into our general conversation. He was a nice guy and understood what we were doing. His job was to stay by the chopper pad all day. Anyone coming up to the pad would tell him where they wanted to go and he would get on the horn (radio) and ask if there was any air traffic in the area going in that direction and ask if it could land and pick the person up. He was sort of like a doorman in a fancy hotel calling cabs; only instead of cabs he would call you a chopper. He suggested we go to a doctor or something. He told us we had to come up with some reason to be at LZ Ross so we could check in with someone official and get on his list. Then we could get on the list at the transient tent so our names would not come up missing that night; we would not be AWOL. I remembered what happened to me when I got dusted and ended up on the missing list.

Of course we had no idea where to go or what to do, so the Spec-4 suggested we could go to the dentist, but he wouldn't recommend it. He said the guy was a butcher, a real geek. He was known as the "Tooth Fairy." The day wore on and that painful memory of my returning to the company after being dusted off and being on the missing list hung over me like a black cloud. I told Jack my story and we both started to worry. We were determined not to go back to our company that day and the dentist started to sound good. We could go and see him; we were sure he could find a cavity or two in our mouths and fill them. That would get us on his list, which would get us on the transient tent list, which would keep us from being reported AWOL. Everybody from the new first sergeant prick to our company commander would know what we were doing but it was by the book. Besides, what could they do? Send us to Vietnam or out to a line company? The one advantage to being on the bottom of the totem pole was that the higher ups ran out of things to threaten you with. We had a plan.

The dentist hut was a half-mile walk away. It seemed to be set by itself along the perimeter road. The Spec-4 from the chopper pad had given us directions. He had also told us where the transient tent was and the directions to a small bar some GIs had set up. I wish we had thought to ask about the bar sooner. But first things first, so we found the dentist hut and walked in.

In less than five minutes we were both walking out the door holding white gauze in our mouths and bloody teeth in our hands. The dentist had made no attempt to fill our teeth or look for any cavities. I'm not sure if he even had any tools to fix teeth. He seemed to have earned his name by ripping out any tooth you complained about and handing you the bloody tooth on your way out, I suppose so you could put it under your pillow that night. He had given me a shot of Novocain first, then Jack, then immediately came back to me before the Novocain had a chance to take effect and ripped out one of my back molars with what seemed to be an ordinary pair of pliers. Then he reached into Jack's mouth, snagged one of his teeth with his pliers, and tore it out.

After we both had been what seemed to us as violated, we were told to leave and started walking down the hot and dusty perimeter road, each of us with a bloody tooth in our hand. We made our way to the transient tent and checked in, got on the list, and headed to the bar. We had paid a high price to get there—two perfectly good teeth—and we intended to make the best of it. It turned out to be not exactly a bar. There were some makeshift tables and the beer was warm, no ice that day, but it would do nicely. We got a couple of beers and started to put them away. We had mentioned to the bartender that we had seen the Tooth Fairy that day and everybody in the place laughed. They all opened their mouths to show their missing teeth. There happened to be a group of Australian soldiers in the bar; Aussies liked to drink. Jack got talking with them, telling them he just got back from their homeland, and he was treated like a long-lost brother.

After the bar closed we went back to the transient tent and it was empty; we had it all to ourselves. We were going to spend one last night living the good life. Things had turned out pretty good that day after all, considering how it had started with that new first sergeant prick on our ass. We had outsmarted that lifer bastard and had not been forced to go out to the field, at least that day. I took my boots off; that's something you don't get to do in the field. My mouth still hurt where the Tooth Fairy had yanked out my permanent rear molar but the bleeding had mostly stopped. Jack had a tape player and he played some music by The Doors. It was a beautiful tropical night and I pleasantly drifted off to sleep listening to Jim Morrison.

I jumped with the first explosion. Jack yelled out to me, "Robo," and threw me the M-16 I had carelessly left by his cot. All I was wearing was my underwear—no shoes, nothing. Some zappers, suicide squads that attacked large bases with satchel charges strapped to their bodies, had raided the base and must have pierced the perimeter right where the transient tent was set up.

I couldn't believe it. This was probably the first time this firebase had been attacked in a year, and these gooks had to do it tonight. And they broke through right in front of our tent. There were about seven of them. They had blown up a bunker on the perimeter and were running down the perimeter road when they happened on us. They had us pinned down behind some sandbags. We had only one clip each in the M-16s we carried. We put the selector switch on semi-auto and fired back, one shot at a time. We heard them talking; there seemed to be an argument going on and they took off running down the road in the direction they were going when they stopped to kill us. As we waited behind the sandbags to see what was going to happen next we figured the zappers decided to get on with their mission and not waste any more time killing a couple of nobodies. We got into an underground bunker that was near the tent and spent the rest of the night there.

In the morning we got dressed and walked down the road toward the chopper pad, in the same direction the zappers had gone the night before. We didn't think too much of what happened to the gooks; we assumed they were dead. We figured with the odds at 400-to-7, even these base camp pussies could kill seven VC. We were wrong. As we got close to the chopper pad we saw a commotion going on. We asked what was happening and were told two of the VC from the zapper team were still alive and holding out in an outcropping of large rocks located on a small rise. The rocks were completely inside the perimeter, in full view of everybody, and I guess the gooks had held off all night long.

I couldn't help but feel sorry for the gooks. I felt how scared and alone they must have felt; how sick is that. I realized I'd better leave the field for good or get back to the company fast because feeling bad for gooks was dangerous. Dogs must have been brought in because I could see two German shepherds running up toward the rocks to rout out the gooks. It didn't take long. The gooks tried to shoot the dogs and exposed themselves enough to get shot. It seemed like everybody in the entire base was there shooting at them. I am surprised none of our own troops got hurt with all the lead flying around. I think a lot of these REMFs were trying to get a shot in because they had never really shot at a live VC. I felt like saying come with us; you will get plenty of chances. They are probably telling their war story today, about the time they killed two VC zappers.

Feelings of R&R love were over for both of us. We'd had our little adventure, our rebellious stand against the new first sergeant prick. I felt the zapper attack was a sign from God, those VC choosing the one night we were there and the exact spot where we were sleeping to break through the perimeter. I could feel my time humping in the bush wasn't over and I was going to have to go back and face what seemed to be my destiny.

KILLER

I never knew his name, he was just known as "Killer" to everybody. He got his name because of his willingness to execute anyone—man, woman, or child—that the company wanted dead. He was about twenty-five but looked a lot older.

The first time I became aware of Killer was when we were on a company move. The whole company would move as one from one location to another. At the new location the company would set up a perimeter and send out patrols from each platoon in different directions. Because of the way we worked, I didn't see a lot of other platoons; we always maintained a distance. That way one incoming mortar round wouldn't kill too many men at once. If a lot of men were killed or injured at once, the enemy could take advantage of the situation and the whole company could be overrun and everybody would be killed. It was a lesson learned the hard way, like everything else in Vietnam.

One day during a company move, the point team came upon a couple of VC who were caught sleeping. They had probably been up all night trying to infiltrate our night position or, worse, mortar some GI position. These guys were screwed. The ARVN interpreter was brought up to the point. Because we were the point squad I could see everything that was going on. The interpreter started yelling at the gooks. He would slap them in the face, and scream at them again. I couldn't understand the words, but anybody watching could understand what was going on. The VC weren't talking. I have a problem being in these situations. I have no sympathy for the gooks, but I can't help feeling bad for another human being in this situation. These guys got caught sleeping, in broad daylight, by an entire infantry company. There was no way out.

The VC weren't talking, so the lieutenant got on the radio and called for Killer. A short time later I saw this guy coming toward us, passing everybody holding in their positions until the word came to move. He looked like the rest of us—tired, worn-out and dirty—and he didn't move very well. He had no athletic ability, no bounce in his step. He just staggered along, passing each soldier one at a time until he got to the point. When he got to the place where the two VC were being held, he was told they wouldn't talk and to kill one, either one. With absolutely no expression on his face, he raised his M-16 and shot the guy on the right in the face, taking out the back of his head. The other VC started talking. The lieutenant wrote down a bunch of stuff the VC was saying through the interpreter. When the VC had said everything the lieutenant wanted to hear, the lieutenant turned to Killer and told him to kill the VC, and he did. The bodies were rolled off the trail and we moved on. This guy would kill on demand, with no hesitation. I could see he was considered to be an asset to the company and was treated with respect by the command.

By this time I had seen a lot of killing and had done enough of my own, but this was murder. I remember thinking this guy must not believe in God. How did he expect to answer for this crime when he died and sat in the presence of God to be judged? This was no idle thought; my friends and I discussed this a lot, and it was important to us to kill fast and without mercy, but still not to murder. I know it's a thin line, and it sure doesn't get clearer as time goes on, but it's like the definition of pornography. I may not be able to describe the difference between art and pornography, but I sure can tell when I see it. That's how it is between killing and murder; it's hard to define but I can tell the difference when I see it.

After that I kept an eye on Killer. His services were used from time to time by the company. We arrived at a fire support base some time later where it was relatively safe. We could move about freely, and would not necessarily draw fire by getting together in small groups. I took this opportunity to talk to Killer one night. I wanted to know what a psychopath thought about life and other things in general. My discussions with him turned out to be much worse than I imagined. He was nice; he had no rage about the VC, or even anger. He even said he liked the Vietnamese people and wouldn't mind coming back after the war to visit. His father owned a car repair garage somewhere in the Midwest. The plan was for him to go back home and take the garage business over and let his father retire.

He went on, with my prodding, telling me how he was going into politics when he got back. I remember him telling me that a man's car is the second biggest investment he makes in life, and he'll vote for anyone he trusts to repair that investment. Killer's plan was to first become mayor of his town. He felt because of his position as a businessman and war hero, he was sure to win. He explained to me that once he got into office he would be in a position of influence. He felt everybody wanted to know the mayor and everybody wanted a favor. He figured with his influence with the town council and zoning board, he would be in a position to supply that favor, for a fee. He told me that after a couple of terms as mayor, he would be old enough and have enough money put away, from all his favors, to go into state politics. He ended by saying, "Who knows where I can go from there?"

I remember it was over one hundred degrees that night, even after sundown, and at the end of our conversation I felt cold because I was in the presence of evil. Not just a chill because of what he said, but cold because I realized I was talking to a man without a soul. I had no idea this type of person existed, someone completely without human feelings, unencumbered by guilt or fear of consequences for his actions. He was obviously getting preferential treatment because of his willingness to commit murder. He had been moved to the company CP in the center of the perimeter, the safest location. He didn't have to pull guard duty at night and didn't go out on platoon-size patrols, unless he was needed for his services. At the time, it seemed like his plan was working, and it seemed like his political career made perfect sense, too.

A few months later, on my twenty-first birthday, we were mortared at night and two of my friends were hit by shrapnel. I helped carry them to the chopper pad. On one side the bodies were stacked up, and on the other side the wounded were waiting to be put on incoming choppers. The head medic performed triage, separating the more seriously wounded to be sent out first from the less seriously wounded who could wait for the next chopper. After I helped put my friends, Micky and Kibby on the chopper, I saw Killer in the group of wounded who were waiting for the next chopper. He had taken shrapnel in the leg. I immediately thought, "He is now going home as a wounded war hero."

After that first chopper came in, loaded up, and took off, the mortaring started up again. The gooks must have been waiting for the dust-off, knowing this would show them just where the center of our perimeter was, and they started dropping mortars on the LZ. After the incoming fire stopped, I saw Killer on my next trip with wounded to the LZ. I could see he had been hit again in the chest and face, and he was now in the group of more seriously wounded going out on the next chopper. When the next chopper came in and loaded up, with Killer on it, it couldn't get any height when it tried to take off. It must have been overloaded with all the wounded. The chopper took off from the top of the hill and came over our position on the side of the hill, losing altitude as it moved. This is what it had to do to gain enough air speed to get the lift it needed to gain altitude. As it dipped down in front of our position, I saw tracer rounds from enemy automatic fire hitting the chopper from both sides. I knew Killer was on that chopper and I could see the tracer rounds going inside the chopper doors, probably hitting the wounded piled on the floor. I had the feeling God wanted Killer to answer for his crimes sooner than Killer planned.

I have no way of knowing if Killer lived or not; somehow the information about what happened to the wounded never got back to us. I am not sure if there was a plan not to tell us, or if it's due to the fact that the wounded were sent to different hospitals, even to Japan. We rarely ever found out what happened to our wounded after we put them on choppers. I hope this guy didn't get back to his hometown to carry out his plan. The last thing this world needs is another homicidal killer in a position of power.

"It is an illusion that youth is happy, an illusion of those who have lost it; but the young know they are wretched for they are full of the truth less ideal which have been instilled into them, and each time they come in contact with the real, they are bruised and wounded".

<u>W. Somerset Maugham</u>, *'Of Human Bondage', 1915*
English dramatist & novelist (1874—1965)

TWENTY-FIRST BIRTHDAY

On my twenty-first birthday, April 4, 1969, I got into five firefights. The first one started when it was still dark out and our platoon was going out on a predawn patrol. We didn't even get twenty feet out of the company perimeter when the shooting started; they must have been waiting for us. The rest of the firefights are a blur, but I remember counting them so I could tell someone, someday, I got in five firefights on my twenty-first birthday. Well, I guess I just told someone.

That night we got mortared. During a break in the incoming rounds I ran over to my other machine gun position to see how they were. Two of my guys, friends, were lying on the ground. Both had been hit in the stomach. Kibby was trying to stuff his guts back in, telling me he would be all right if I could just get him to the chopper so he could go on the R&R he had coming up in a few days. Mickey was my best friend. He pleaded with me to check and see if his dick was still attached to his body; he couldn't feel anything down there. I fumbled around to see. It was so dark I couldn't see anything and when I tried to feel—he was really insistent I feel—it was all a gooey mess. I lied to him and told him he was all right, but he was unconscious by then. I helped carry both of them up to a rallying point—one pile for the dead, one pile for the wounded to be taken out first when a dust-off got there. Then I went back to my foxhole and started to dig it deeper; I was afraid the mortars would start again. It started raining very hard and I remember getting cold. I looked at my watch and noticed it was after midnight. It had been a hell of a twenty-first birthday. Phil Stein died that night, another good friend of mine. I still keep a rubbing of his name taken from The Wall. Someone else went and got it; I couldn't.

SILLY BILLY

I met Billy in a bar fight at our company's first stand-down. We hadn't been with the company more than a couple of weeks and most of us green seeds were unsure of ourselves and kept a low profile. Not Billy; I could hear him in the next room screaming at another guy about a hooker in a local village.

I went into the bar room of the Chu Lai Hilton and saw two guys engaged in a loud argument about who was the girl's boyfriend. Billy was short and stocky and enraged. He was warning the other guy to stay away, and when he stopped yelling to take a breath and the other guy started to yell, Billy sucker punched him and the guy fell to the floor like a stone. Billy turned around to the bar and asked for another beer, indicating the argument was over.

I couldn't believe what an asshole he was to be fighting over a girl neither of them was ever going to see again, a girl who was for sale for a few bucks. He was entertaining to listen to and as I drank my beer from a distance and listened to him ramble on about this and that in his loud voice, I heard him say he was from Connecticut. Finding someone to talk to from my home state was hard, so even though I thought this guy was a nut, and dangerous to be around, I slid down the bar and struck up a conversation. We talked about home, drank beer, and when the three-day stand-down was over, we each went with different platoons out to the field.

I didn't see Billy again until our platoons worked together on an operation a few months later. Billy was walking point and we came upon a small hooch area. An old man was sleeping in a hammock and Billy killed him with a burst of M-16 fire as the old man lay there. I will never understand why he did that.

A few days later someone told me Billy got hurt in a fire-fight and was dusted off. Later Billy told me what had happened. He had been walking point again and came to an old French plantation. These old estates were plentiful, and a reminder of what Vietnam was like before the war started—beautiful.

Vietnam must have been a paradise in the true meaning of the word—a garden, full of tropical flowers and fountains and huge villas with thick adobe-like walls. These abandoned villas were favorite hiding places for both the Viet Cong and the Americans; they offered good protection in the main house, always had a good source of water, and the walls of the court-yards provided good protection for a perimeter. It seems our company commander sent Billy's platoon to check out this villa for a night lager.

Billy told me he was real nervous about going into the villa. Something didn't feel right; he was obsessed that morning about booby traps and trip wires, and kept watching the ground for them. He said he and Red, his M-79 back-up man, had gotten into the courtyard and were walking through the garden toward the main house, scanning the path for trip wires. Red was a tall redheaded kid from someplace like Texas. I remember they looked like Mutt and Jeff together.

Billy said just as he came near the main house, he was look-ing at the ground and saw a pair of rubber sandals, gook shoes. He looked up and there, about ten feet away, was a Viet Cong staring at him and holding an AK-47. He thinks the gook must also have been looking at the ground and they both looked up at the same time.

Billy said his M-16 was at his hip and he pulled the trigger and started firing and turned and started running at the same time. Red was right behind Billy, saw what happened, and leveled the loaded M-79 grenade launcher to fire over Billy's head at the gook. Billy didn't know Red was so close and ran head first into him, putting off his aim. Red fired the high explosive grenade round and it hit a stone wall. It missed the gook but the shrapnel got both Billy and Red. They had shot themselves. I believed him; a guy doesn't make up a story like that.

Billy said he got as far as a Saigon hospital. His only real injury, except for a lot of minor lacerations, was a deep wound in his shoulder, and it was healing much too soon for his liking. He was getting used to the clean living of hospital patient life and didn't want to go back to the field.

He said he shammed it up (pretended to be injured) pretty good. He found some bandages and wrapped up his shoulder with a big ball of white gauze, hiding in the system of the big Army hospital in Saigon. At a casual glance, he looked like any other recuperating GI. He joined up with another guy from our company, George, who had been injured in another firefight, and the two of them were living it up.

All good things come to an end. One day a doctor came into the day room where they were watching TV—a doctor they had never seen before—and demanded to see their wounds. He took off the bandages and saw their nearly healed scars. Billy figured someone had ratted them out. The jig was up and they were discharged within the hour with orders to go back to Chu Lai, to their company, and back to the field.

Billy figured since he and George were already in Saigon, why not stay awhile and see the sights? A month later he and George were still in Saigon and finally gave themselves up to the MPs for being AWOL. They knew the MPs were after them and had stories of being chased down alleys by the MPs in Saigon. The authorities sent them back to Chu Lai under guard, where they were to stand trial by court-martial for being AWOL. The CO could have brought them up on charges of desertion but he must have figured they were in Saigon for legitimate wounds so he would leave it an AWOL.

This is where I come back into the story. While Billy and George were waiting for their court-martial, they were sent back to the field and George was assigned to our platoon. George was a real nice guy; he smoked a lot of dope but he kept us in tears telling us stories about Billy and him in Saigon. All the stories were about drinking, smoking, and the different women they had. We were so desperate for entertainment we didn't care if the stories were true or not.

I took George aside one time and asked him how he and Billy did all the stuff he talked about without any money—booze, dope, and women all cost money. He said they had plenty of money at first. Billy would just call his father in Connecticut and his father would send him money through the Red Cross. He said that's why they turned themselves in; Billy's father smelled a rat and stopped sending him money.

Billy took another path. When he was told to go back to the field he proclaimed he was a conscientious objector and re-fused to go back. When I heard about this I thought about the old man he killed in the hammock. They threw him in jail and gave him a lawyer. It seems all of Billy's family—his mother, father, and grandparents on both sides—were Seventh Day Adventists, who did have a history of conscientious objection. The Army doesn't give up easily; they took him out of jail, gave him a first aid kit, and told him he was now a non-combatant medic. He was sent out to the field with a personal MP at his side to make sure he didn't get lost. He spent most of the time up on the hill at an aid station.

George died a few weeks later. He went out on a patrol and didn't come back. I am sure I was told at the time what happened but I can't remember any of the details. That's how it would happen—if you weren't personally there, a guy just died in a firefight, got dusted off, and you never heard about it or him again. Deep down you were just glad it wasn't you.

I didn't see Billy again until my last stand-down. After the stand-down some other guys from the battalion who were going home and I were told to mount up to the back of truck that was going to take us to the airport in Chu Lai, the first leg of our trip home. Billy came around the corner and hopped up on the truck and sat down. We all started talking about how we never expected to live to this day and how nice it was going to do, not have to think about going back to the field and facing the VC again. We were all very excited and there was an overall feeling of well-being.

A clerk showed up with a list of names, checking us off to make sure we all had the correct orders. When he saw Billy he was taken aback. I will never forget what he said. "What are you doing up there? You aren't going anywhere." Billy started yelling, "What do you mean, I came with these guys a year ago and I am going home with them." He turned around to get our support. The clerk said in a detached voice, "Yeah, but they didn't take a month's vacation in Saigon. Get off the truck." Billy kept yelling like a madman but he knew he had lost, and finally got off. I remember him arguing with the clerk, saying that the court-martial was called off. The clerk replied that just meant he didn't go to jail; he still had to make up the time. That's the last I saw of Billy for a while.

About four months later, after my leave at home, I was assigned to Fort Jackson, South Carolina. One day as I was going into the mess hall I saw one of the guys from my old company,

Black Death. He was about three months behind me in rotation so he had just gotten back. After we caught up a bit I asked if he knew what had happened to Billy. I told him what happened when we were leaving and the clerk took him off the truck. He stopped smiling and told me what had happened.

He said it must have been that same day, the day we left and Billy didn't, that he happened to be on the hill, meaning LZ Center, and waiting for a chopper out to the company in the field. He said a Chinook came and landed and two MPs dragged a guy off the back ramp of the chopper. The guy's hands were handcuffed behind his back and he was in new fatigues. He said he didn't know it was Billy but learned his name later. He said the guy was acting so crazy the MPs seemed afraid to uncuff his hands and just left him lying in the dirt, cussing and spitting, saying he was going to kill them when he got loose. A crowd began to form and the Chinook seemed to be waiting for the MPs, so they uncuffed him and quickly jumped into the chopper and took off. Joe said an officer came over to Billy and said he just got off the radio with Billy's top sergeant and was told to make sure Billy got out to the company in the field and under no circumstance was he to stay on the hill.

Joe said this is where it got weird. Billy looked at the officer, took off all his clothes—shoes, socks, everything—and threw them at the officer. Billy said, "Fuck you," turned and walked off the hill. No clothes, shoes, food, water, weapon, nothing. Joe said by the time he got back to the company that day they were all talking about the guy who told some officer to get fucked and took off his clothes and walked off the hill.

Joe found out later that Billy had gone to an ARVN aid station on some small hill in the middle of nowhere. He heard weeks later a company patrol saw Billy walking down a trail once, looking like he didn't have a care in the world. He said they almost shot him because he was dressed like a gook, but he didn't run when he saw them so they didn't shoot. He just said hi as he passed by and kept on his way. Joe said he heard Billy just showed up on LZ Center one day, saying it was time for him to go home. He got on a chopper and left.

As luck would have it Billy showed up at Fort Jackson a month later. I couldn't wait to ask him if this story was true. He seemed a little embarrassed that I knew about it and said there was no way he was going back to the company. He laughed when I asked about him throwing his clothes at the officer, but he didn't deny it. He said he found the ARVN aid station by accident. When I pressed him about what he did there, he said he was high for the whole month and only got straight once in a while to walk to a village, for women, where he would stay for a few days and then go back to the ARVN station.

About a month later, on a Sunday morning, a clerk from my new company's orderly room came into my barracks and woke me, telling me I had an emergency phone call. I got dressed real fast and ran to the phone. It was Billy, telling me he was in jail in town and could I come and get him out.

PART VIII

LAST FIVE DAYS IN THE FIELD

"None but a coward dares to boast that he has never known fear".

Ferdinand Foch

French general (1851—1929)

BEGINNING OF THE END

I will now try to—I'm not sure what—explain, confess, relive, or just put on paper the experience of my last five days in the field. Remembering what happened in excruciating detail is not the problem. The details are daily in my thoughts. I push them out of the way each day so I can think about the tasks at hand and get through the day, but these thoughts are my default way of thinking. If at anytime during the day I slow down, or go into reverse, these events I am about to disclose jump into my conscience.

I was a week away from my DEROS date. For me, my DEROS date was the worst day of my life and my best day—June 3. When you arrive in Vietnam, that day becomes your DEROS day. You go home 365 days from the day you arrive in country, your DEROS day. Everybody knows when their DEROS day is, and everybody knows how many days they have to go before their DEROS day arrives. It becomes your sole reason to go on.

As a grunt, it's the carrot on the end of the stick. It's the reason you don't shoot your platoon sergeant, platoon leader, company commander, or anybody who gets in the way of you making it to your DEROS date. Shooting any one of them would only land you in LBJ, and if you go there, your DEROS date gets put on hold until you come out, and the time starts counting again. Now if shooting any one of them would make it more likely for you to make it to your DEROS, go for it. There was an unwritten code between grunts that we would not kill each other to get to DEROS, but I found that line got blurred as I came closer to mine. The concept of being a good soldier and facing the enemy for the good of the country or any other reason soon becomes a totally abstract thought, not having any bearing on your present situation. So I was one week away from my DEROS date.

When I first joined the company, a short-timer was someone with six or seven months in the field and he was always pulled out of the field, the idea being that he had done his part and was now too nervous to do the unit any good in the field. He would be given a simple job in the rear to complete his tour, so as not to become a hazard to the men around him. Officers stayed in the field only about three months, long enough to get their CIBs (combat infantry badges), then went off to the rear as finance officers or some other safe job, lazily letting their DEROS date come to them, not fighting for each day, and sometimes each hour, hoping against hope they might make it home. I hate them for that. I hate those guys who tell people they were in Vietnam, even tell people they were in the field, fought in the jungle. I never saw or heard of anyone spending his whole twelve months in the field, with a line unit the whole time. I feel I got fucked. We were told it took seven people in the rear doing their jobs to support each person in the field. I wanted one of those jobs. It was made clear to me I was not going to get one of those jobs. Things were different now, and I was going to stay in the field until I got dusted off or DEROSed out.

So there I was, seven days from DEROS and I was still in the field, going into the biggest battle I had ever been in. We were told a Special Forces camp out on the flatlands had been overrun by a large number of regular NVA forces. The gooks had killed everybody and were now occupying the camp. We were going to take the hill back. It was a huge operation, requiring I don't know how many battalions of the Americal Division.

Our part was to join up with some track units, supply them with flank security while we moved toward the twin hills base that was the Special Forces camp, and retake the hills. We had never worked with tanks before and it was awkward to get used to. They did everything in a grand scale compared to the infantry. I don't know how many troops of tracks there were, but there were about one hundred vehicles altogether. A troop is what a company of tracks is called. A track is any tracked vehicle: tank, APC (armored personnel carrier), mine sweepers, Zippo units (napalm flame throwers), or any other version of tracked vehicle they had come up with to kill gooks—all deadly if your eyes were slanted.

The first day was wild. One hundred tracks got on line and started moving forward, shooting all the time. We followed behind them looking for caves or anything they missed. It all seemed very messy and uncoordinated to me, but they kept going until lunch. These guys actually stopped at noon and had lunch. They pulled into a big circle like covered wagons. Then a Chinook chopper landed in the center of the circle and shut down its engines, parking there. The cook crew came out and set up serving tables and served the whole outfit hot food just cooked at their base camp and kept in warmers until it was served. After lunch the cook crew packed up and the Chinook took off. The tracks reassembled their battle line and the afternoon portion of the battle resumed.

The next day things didn't go as well. We had come out of the jungle and elephant grass onto a great dry rice paddy. When rice paddies were dry they were as hard as concrete and as flat as a frozen lake; it looked like a huge playing field. That day the NVA weren't playing. They must have gotten tired of getting their asses kicked the day before and were looking for some payback. Because we were in open rice paddies, the grunts couldn't keep up, so we were told to mount the tracks. We were not on line anymore. There was no shooting; we were just riding along in a mob. I was staring straight ahead when I saw the first RPG (rocket propelled grenade) hit the hard ground just in front of us. It bounced off the ground and hit a track to our front and right. The slow motion kicked in again as our world exploded and we jumped off the track. There were six thousand NVA in the jungle around us and we rode right into their trap. There wouldn't be any lunch break today.

It was a complete mess. The infantry was totally exposed, with no cover, and the tanks must have been trained to keep moving so they wouldn't be easy targets. A lot of grunts were run over by our tracks, mostly when they backed up, not knowing the infantry were huddled in back of them for some kind of cover. We were close to the jungle on the rice paddy and our track turned toward the jungle and opened fire. We ran behind the track for cover and I put my machine gun down on the ground and lay down for a better position to fire from. The track suddenly jumped back, catching my machine gun under its steel tracks, and I rolled out of the way just in time or I would have been crushed like so many others. The track took off and we were left there, totally exposed to enemy fire and with no place to hide. I didn't even have a gun.

This other guy, Sergeant Moore, and I ran together to a small dike about a foot high. It provided some cover but we were afraid a tank would run over us, so we kept poking our heads up to see if one was coming. The whole rice paddy was now a mess of one hundred tracks running around firing wildly. Helicopter gunships were shooting up the tree lines, and in our little world we were trying not to get splattered. I felt a sting and thought I had been shot. Then another, and then a lot more, and I realized we were lying in a bee's nest. As I slapped the bees and tried to squirm out of their way, a real bullet hit just above my head and I stopped moving. Another hit and I looked up to see where it came from and saw a gook not fifty yards away, kneeling in the grass on the edge of the rice paddy aiming right at me. He seemed to be smiling.

I had no weapon and the gook could see me panic as I called out to Sergeant Moore to shoot the gook. Sergeant Moore had no chance of hearing me, so I grabbed the muzzle of his M-16, trying to pull it away from him so I could shoot the NVA soldier. Of course he resisted, so I started to kick him in the head as hard as I could, hearing another round miss my ear by an inch. He fought like a badger but I had knocked off his helmet with the first kick and I was now working on the top of his head and his face with the heel of my boot. I was afraid to look up at the gook. He had all the time in the world to kill me, and I didn't want to see the smirk on his face as he put one between my eyes. I was literally kicking the shit out of Sergeant Moore and I still seemed to have plenty of time to watch out for tanks coming at us and to flinch every time a bee stung me. When I finally looked up, the gook was gone. All I saw was a wall of flame and a Zippo tank that had just lit up the tree line with napalm. The battle was starting to turn in our favor and all the tracks started to move away, so Sergeant Moore and I got up and started running in the direction the tracks were going, not wanting to be left behind. His face was all bloody and he kept looking at me in total bewilderment. We were running for our lives and there was no extra breath for conversation but I am sure he never had a clue what had been going on. I never saw him again to explain.

The tracks finally got us to the base of the twin hills that was the Special Forces camp. The NVA had retreated off the hill and let us stroll up and make ourselves at home. Tracks don't climb hills, even hills this small, so they took off. An hour after we had heard the last tracks roar off, the NVA moved in around the hill and surrounded us—six thousand of them against two hundred fifty of us. I had four days left to my DEROS date.

By this time I had stopped talking to anyone except when necessary and they had stopped talking to me. I found myself a small slit trench with just enough room for me. I stayed there and didn't come out until the next morning, when I had to come out for a patrol. There were two dead bodies in the trench that I hadn't noticed at first—that probably accounted for all the flies. I didn't care about the dead bodies in my foxhole or the other guys or anything. It's not that I didn't have any emotions; it's just that they had run out. My emotion allotment had run out and I moved around like a zombie. Now I was the undead.

We had constant artillery supporting us, and gun-ships and F-4 jets and anything else the higher command could throw at the enemy. Otherwise the NVA would just come back up the hill, kill us all, and have lunch. At night a fixed-wing C-130 came at sundown and started firing a Mini-gun while circling our position on the hill. After about forty-five minutes another one would show up and take over. The night was lit up with flares, always two or three in the air on all sides of the hill, gently floating down on their little parachutes. This went all night long until morning. The other air support started again when the sun came up. The NVA must not have wanted to retake the hill, because I felt they could have overrun us at any time but there was never a big frontal assault, just constant probing and harassing fire. I think they were just using us for bait, keeping up the heat for some reason. Who knew? Gooks...

It was insanity to go off the hill on a patrol. What were we looking for? The NVA were there, all you had to do was look; they weren't even trying to hide very much. But the colonel wanted a patrol and our platoon was picked to go. For all I knew, other platoons were going out on patrols on the other side of the hill. I didn't know and didn't care. I just wanted to stay in my hole with my new foxhole buddies and somehow live for the next few days until my DEROS date. We went down the hill and as soon as we got to the base we heard a .50-caliber barking off and I dropped to the ground looking for cover. It seemed like the other guys around me were on another patrol, not the one I was on. They looked down at me like I was crazy. They didn't seem to know what a .50-caliber sounded like, or had no idea what it could do if used against us. Its bullets go through anything—trees, ground, even rock. It just explodes the rock you are hiding behind.

A gunship showed up and started firing. We had popped smoke to show our position and the gunship hovered over us shooting at the .50-caliber and its crew. This wasn't a converted Huey gunship, but a Cobra. It was only thirty-six inches wide, with the gunner in front and the pilot in back. It had rocket tubes on its short wings, machine guns next to the tubes, and was built around a Minigun that fired so fast the sound was a blur. This was a killing machine, but it seemed to be taking in more fire than it was giving out. It got lower over our position, hoping to get a better angle to take out the .50-caliber. Black smoke came out of the back and it started to spin out of control, threatening to come down on our heads. I started to run out of the way and it started to fall in the direction I was running. I stopped and started to run back, looking up, and it seemed to follow me whichever direction I took. By now, it was starting to break up in the air and parts were falling on our heads, probably the turbine tearing itself apart. It finally came down in a big ball of fire. I started to go back up the hill and others followed.

The new lieutenant this time was called "Lumpy," for some reason, and he was afraid of me. He must have heard a lot of stories in officer school about grunts fragging (enlisted men killing their officers). I figured he saw me as a prime candidate for fragging his ass and he gave me a wide berth. He probably was looking forward to my leaving the company. Unfortunately, he was more afraid of the colonel who was watching this farce from the hill above us. The colonel was in radio contact with him and told him to take his platoon and "get that gun," meaning the .50-caliber that shot down the gunship. The lieutenant called out to me to stop and said the colonel says we have to get the gun. I turned and looked at him and suddenly felt sorry for him. He had this colonel up on the hill telling him to do stupid things, like get this .50-caliber gun that just shot down a gunship, and they give him people like me to get the job done. I would not only disobey him if I could, I would kill him if I thought it would get me home. He was a nice guy and I probably would have liked him, but he was in the wrong business; this place would kill him.

I had no choice but to turn around with my men and go try to get the gun. There were too many witnesses to do anything else. I was willing to go to LBJ for a while if it meant I would get out of this mess, even though my time would start again when I got out and I only had a few days left. But if I disobeyed a direct order, under fire, with the colonel watching and in front of everybody in the platoon and everybody watching on the hill, I would probably be sent to Fort Leavenworth to do hard labor. When you are in a combat situation you have to make a decision fast, list all your options and take action. If an option had been to tie Lumpy's hands behind his back, knock him to the ground and choke him to death with my bare hands, looking into his eyes as his life drained from his body, I would have done it. Luckily for Lumpy, that was not on my list of options that day.

We went to get the gun. I fully expected to be cut down by

the .50-caliber as soon as we got close to it, but we had lucked out. The gunship that got shot down started a fire and the smoke from the burning underbrush gave us cover to get close to the gun. The gooks were taking the gun apart, probably to move it because its position was known, and didn't see us coming. We quickly killed most of them and set a large amount of C-4 explosives and blew it up. We blindfolded the prisoners, the ones from the gun team we didn't kill, and started back up the hill. I will never know why, but the point team going back up the hill moved very slowly—green seeds. I ran past the point team and ran flat out up the rest of the hill and jumped into the first bunker I came to. Just as I landed in the bunker, on some other guys, the mortars started and hit a lot of the platoon and other guys standing on the hill. Did they think this was a sport? Did they not want to seem to be afraid in front of other men? When the mortars eased off I made my way back to my hole. My foxhole buddies were there.

That night went like the last one. I tried to sleep but the two rotting corpses I was bunking with seemed to be attracting a lot of rats at night, and between the rats and the constant flares and the shooting, I just couldn't seem to get much sleep.

MY LAST PATROL

The next morning Lumpy came over to my position and told me we were going to have to go out on another patrol. He had to squat down to talk to me because even though there was absolutely nothing happening on the hill at the time, I wouldn't come out of my hole. Looking back now, I can see I was really becoming unhinged. His expression was odd when he tried to talk. The incredible stench of the rotting bodies was making his eyes water, but he never said a thing about me lying there in a trench with about a thousand flies covering me and the corpses.

He patiently explained to me that he had tried to get me out of this patrol, because I was so short, but the captain would not hear of it. He explained how our platoon and another platoon (we had so many losses we needed two platoons for a patrol) were going to set up a box position at the base of the hill. We'd move out about a hundred yards, maintaining the box so we kept a perimeter at all times, and then move back up to the hill and that would be that. He then told me the big news. Because we had lost so many men, our company was going to be extracted the next day, brought back to Chu Lai, have a stand-down, and be re-supplied and get a bunch of replacements. He knew this meant I would leave the field with the company and I would never come back to the field again.

It was very nice of him to take the time to tell me all this. I never said a word. I might have nodded but I am not sure. The undead don't talk much. I really did not want to go on this patrol. I could feel myself losing my grip on reality; my mind seemed to slip into dreams when I was wide-awake.

I was really scared. Up until this point I hadn't allowed myself to think about the possibility of actually going home. I kept it away from my conscious thoughts, always thinking about the task at hand. On the trail I kept thinking where I would jump if we got hit, kept looking down the trail to see where my next cover would be. Where could the gooks be hiding? Was that a booby trap? Did I have enough water to make it through the night or the next day if needed? I kept the idea of really going home out of my mind, as a myth, the "World." But now the myth was almost here. The reality of going home rushed in on me. I started to think I was going to make it, just one more patrol. Lumpy did say I would be in the back, and we wouldn't be going far, just out one hundred yards and back up the hill and then home. After all I had been through, all the disappointments I had, I must have made a giant leap of faith to actually think things would be that easy.

We went down the hill, my gun in the rear of the line. We set up the square as planned and again my gun was in the rear, the safe position. A short way out word was passed back to me that the forward machine gun was jammed and I would have to bring my machine gun up to the forward position. Somehow I wasn't surprised. I started moving my gun up with my two ammo bearers and my assistant gunner. We were moving up through the center of the box when the gooks sprung their trap. The gooks had been hiding in spider holes in the ground and in the trees. The result of the ambush was that the gooks ended up both inside and outside our box. It was our worst nightmare. Actually, it wasn't so good for the gooks, either.

At first there was a lot of shooting, but then everybody dropped to the ground and everybody on both sides was afraid to fire because we were so close in the tall grass. All you could hear was the wounded crying out. Nobody moved. We carried no water, no food or rucksack, only weapons and all the ammo we could carry. I made my guys carry a lot on this patrol. I wasn't going to get killed on my last patrol because I ran out of ammo. I looked around and couldn't see anything, the grass was too high, but I did see all the shiny new M-60 rounds that we unpacked that morning sitting there on my men's backs, ready to be used. I hadn't fired a shot because we were right in the middle of the box and I was afraid if I shot in any direction I would hit our own troops.

All of a sudden everybody on both sides started a fire at once, it turned into complete chaos. Hand grenades and smoke grenades started to go off and what little visibility we did have was lost. My team and I stumbled towards the open rice paddy, there was no coordinated fire. Nobody knew where anybody else was and helicopter gun-ships flew in and raked the area with random mini-gun fire. I had heard later that the captain had seen our situation from the hill and decided to call in gun-ships and napalm on our own position in an effort to break us free from the NVA that had surrounded us. He felt to do nothing would have just been letting us stay there and die, this way, it leaves some of us might get out through the confusion.

I knew there was an open dry rice paddy. If we made it to the paddy we might regroup and be able to pull back to the hill.

Between us we had about fifteen hundred rounds, a lot of ammo. I kept firing in the same direction. I fired low, cutting down the grass and small trees and brush, not letting anyone go in my path. We kept moving, kept moving forward toward the rice paddy. Finally we broke out of the high grass onto the open paddy and there was a nice drainage ditch we scrambled into. By this time gunships and F-4 Phantoms were all over, blasting away in every direction. We established a firing line in the ditch and started firing at a group of NVA coming toward us, probably trying to get out of the center, too. We were dropping them pretty good when out of the corner of my eye—I still see it as clear as the day it happened—a jet fighter came in real low and dropped napalm right in front of our ditch. I can still see that shiny aluminum canister tumbling down from the sky. My slow motion kicked in and I tried to duck down but I was moving in slow motion, too. In the past when the slow motion started, I could look around and see details clearly, having plenty of time to react or duck. At one point I could see bullets going through the air. I couldn't dodge the bullets but I could see them. This time I was in slow motion, too.

The canister hit the ground and the napalm spilled, instantly bursting into flames. The NVA we were engaged with took a direct hit and they burned up. We were missed by the direct burst of flames. I got some burns and it singed my hair, and the explosion of flame sucked away all the air in the ditch so we couldn't breathe. We ran away from the flames coughing and choking, gasping for air while we rolled on the ground. As soon as we got our breath we started back toward the ditch thirty or forty feet away. Our weapons were still there. More gooks came out of the smoke toward us. I stopped and I am not sure what happened next. Somewhere I decided I had had enough and started running back toward the hill. There were three or four of us running, flat out, up the hill. This was the second machine gun I had lost in the last few days and I was through. I quit.

When we got to the top, I saw the look on the faces of the men standing at the top of the hill watching the firefight going on below. I was gasping for air and in a ball of sweat. I had no helmet, no weapon or ammo, nothing but the T-shirt on my back. My hair and face were burned and I was making garbled animal noises as I pushed past them and ran to my hole. They looked at me funny—not funny *ha, ha.* I didn't even know who these people were or notice their rank. My foxhole buddies didn't mind the state I was in. I didn't leave my hole until the next morning. That night was more of the same—enemy mortar rounds coming in and C-130 gun-ships holding the gooks back from coming up the hill to get us.

The next morning as planned a Chinook came in to extract us. We would normally have been brought out by slicks, but because we were surrounded, and the enemy had so much anti–air fire power, the brass figured a powerful Chinook could fly directly over our position and drop straight down into our perimeter. More importantly for us, it could fly straight up with a full load. A slick taking off from our hill in that hot humid air, with a full load of troops, would have to use all its power just to rise off the ground enough to clear the top of the hill, then fly low over the enemy to gain enough air speed to get lift. Hot air meant less dense air that the helicopter rotor blades could push down against, which meant less lift. In Chu Lai, the re-supply slicks, fully loaded with fuel, supplies and five or six troops, sometimes didn't have enough power to lift off the ground, and would bounce a few times and take off down the runway like a fixed-wing aircraft.

I only explain this to show the position we were in. Our rifle company was over one hundred men strong when we started that operation a few days before. It would have taken three or four Chinooks to carry us out then. Now one hook could take us all out, with enough power to rise straight up.

The big Chinook dropped down, its back ramp already lowered when it touched the ground, and we all scurried in. The other rifle company, the poor bastards left behind, set up its men all around the hill perimeter and started a mad minute when we began to lift. A mad minute is when everyone starts to shoot in an outward direction at the same time for a minute. It's used for different reasons. This morning it was used to try to keep the small arms fire down; keep the gooks' heads down until we got high enough to be above enemy fire. The Chinook had barely touched down when it started up again. I was frozen in fear but also relieved, because I knew one way or another my time in the field was over. If we made it to Chu Lai I was going home. If we got shot down, there was no way I could live through the crash and even if I did the NVA would kill us fast—no time for them to play with F-4 Phantoms overhead. Either way, I had it made.

I could feel the strain of the turbines sending a rough vibration all through the ship. The pilots knew what was at stake and I could feel they were giving it all they could. The expected small arms fire started to hit the ship—*ping, ping*—and I felt the thud of a .50-caliber come up through the floor and go through the roof as we rose higher and higher. The guy across from me took a .50-caliber through the ass and out his back—he was dead by the time he hit the floor. The NVA must have moved in another .50-caliber during the night. Judging by the angle of the rounds coming through the ship, it must have been right beneath us. They probably hoped a chopper would come in and would be easy pickings.

I think my slow motion kicked in again. I could distinctly hear the small arms fire still hitting but with a lot less power as they hit the aluminum body of the ship. The rounds didn't even seem to be coming through anymore, just bouncing off. The .50-caliber had stopped firing altogether; something must have happened to make it stop firing so abruptly. The fresh cool air rushed in through the back of the Chinook. Nothing had smelled so good in a long time. Of course, I had been staying in an open grave with decomposing flesh for the last few days, but that was all over.

PART IX

STAND-DOWN

When the hook landed in Chu Lai I walked down the back ramp and a guy I knew, Billy, was sitting in a jeep in a nice new uniform, with a big trailer full of ice and beer. The ice and beer were for us. Twenty minutes ago I was praying for my life in that chopper, with bullets whizzing through it, and now I was looking at a whole trailer full of ice and beer. I couldn't help but think of those poor unlucky bastards still slugging it out on that hill while we were going to a party. What a war.

This was the start of our company stand-down. The company would stay in the rear for three days, getting re-supplied with replacements, more green seeds, taking the place of guys like me and the dead and injured. At the same time there would be plenty of beer, cigarettes, slant-eyed bands brought in from God knows where, and anything else you could scrounge up. Drugs, prostitutes, stag films—you name it, and someone at the Chu Lai Hilton, as it was called, would supply it for a price.

After I cleaned up I went up to the rec hall. I would have preferred to go someplace else, but we weren't allowed to leave the compound. We were kept in with high fences with razor wire and armed guards at the gates. The guards were not there to keep the gooks out; we were in the center of Chu Lai, which had several separate perimeters around it. The guards were there to keep the drunken grunts in. Our weapons were locked up. The people who ran the Chu Lai Hilton had plenty of experience with line companies in from the field for three days and then going back to work. That's what they did, and not letting us kill each other was part of their job. The other part of their job was not to let the drunken grunts loose on the rest of the population of Chu Lai. These people had a nice clean life. The local gooks did all the hard work while they sat back, drank beer, and waited for their DEROS to come. The last thing they wanted was a bunch of drunken twenty-year-olds running around with loaded automatic weapons with absolutely nothing to lose by shooting somebody.

There were some guys standing at a rough plywood bar; everything smelled of stale beer. The rough shape of the bar and the holes in the walls told the story of company after company spending their stand-downs there. I was still in shock. I got a beer and joined the group standing there. I didn't recognize any of them and assumed they were replacements. They were talking about things in general and probably thought I was also new because I had on new fatigues, a nice haircut (the singed part cut off), and I was talking to them. The other guys in the company seemed to clump together by platoon. Nobody talked to the green seeds—what was the point? Most of them wouldn't be here in a month.

I started to relax. I was having a normal conversation about something other than Nam stuff. These guys had no idea what we had gone through only hours before that same morning, and now I was drinking a beer at the Chu Lai Hilton. I had not talked to any of my comrades about what had happened the day before. My whole being shouted, "Keep away! I am not going to discuss it."

Actually, nobody had talked to me at all, not about the last patrol. They just ignored me altogether, which was fine. Just as I was warming up from the beer and the idea of going home, I heard a loud commotion from the hall. Someone was shouting, "Where's Boyd? Where is that machine gunner from Kelso (the name of our platoon), the one doing all the firing on that last patrol?" I froze. I heard someone say I was in the bar and my face turned bright red as it always does when I get embarrassed. He said he wanted to shake my hand.

A crowd had formed by now—I was devastated. I wasn't sure if my actions the day before were right or wrong, but I sure didn't want to be thanked for saving my own life. He was saying that because I opened fire from inside the ambush, that diversion allowed his platoon a chance to get out themselves.

I bowed out of the bar and the rec hall as soon as I could, pushing through a crowd of well-wishers and backslappers. They undoubtedly thought I was modest about my accomplishments, and I shied away with humiliation. Nothing was farther from the truth. I had shot my way out of the ambush not knowing who was in the way, to save my life. If he thought I had done it to save them, he was wrong.

PART X

GOING HOME

On the plane coming home I was sick. I knew I had malaria again, but if I had gone to the medic at the transportation center in Cameron Bay they would have put me into a hospital for a week or more. I would not let that happen. In processing out of Vietnam they had us sign a paper saying we did not have active malaria at the time. Because it was in my records that I had been hospitalized with malaria, I was looked at closely. They said they didn't want anybody going back to the world (nickname for the United States) with active malaria because a certain mosquito might bite you and could pass the malaria on to someone else. I was willing to take that risk. When my freedom bird (the airplane that brought you home) touched down in Cameron Bay, I was getting in and I wasn't getting out until I was back in the world.

When my plane took off from Vietnam and got airborne, there was only mild clapping. Most of the passengers were Air Force pukes; they hardly seemed to notice we were going home. The few grunts on the plane were too cautious to clap. Disappointment was our way of life—anything could happen. Home was still eight thousand miles away. There was a lot that could happen between now and then. The plane ride home was uneventful, except for a ten-hour layover in Japan. They would not let us off the plane and tucked our bird out of the way in some corner on the tarmac while we waited. No one ever told us why we were waiting. I don't even remember caring. I was going home. When the plane finally landed in Seattle, there was that same mild cheering. I didn't cheer. I was starting to feel something very strong coming alive in me that I had not felt for a long time. Hope.

I started to let myself believe for the first time that I was going to make it. We got off the plane and the Army personnel were herded to their processing center. After another haircut, new Class A dress uniform, and some easy processing including paying us in cash, we were all put on a Greyhound bus, with our airline tickets in hand, to bring us to the airport. Now I was really starting to believe I had made it.

The malaria made me very sick. My fever was coming back and I was seeing double. I couldn't eat and I was so weak, I dragged my feet to the bus. My whole body had the shakes. The jungle rot on my arms and legs, and now my face, had hit its all-time high. The penicillin no longer had any affect and I could feel the puss oozing out of the open sores on my forearms and ruining my nice new khaki shirt. I made a mental note not to take off my new uniform jacket with all the nice new medals on it. I didn't want to be embarrassed by anyone seeing the puss marks bleeding through on my long-sleeved shirt. I never felt so good in my life. I was going home.

The bus made it as far as the main gate. There was a crowd of about two hundred people, civilians. As the bus passed through the gate the crowd surrounded the bus and started screaming at us. I was holding my aching head against the cool glass window. I was looking at the people in the crowd under my window; their faces were angry. I wondered who they were angry at. The girls would have been pretty if their faces weren't twisted with rage. The bus driver said the crowd was big today because it was Saturday and a lot of these people didn't have to go to school or work. It had been a long time since the day of the week had any bearing on my life.

I heard the words "war protesters," but it didn't mean a thing to me. The crowd started to rock the bus and my head bounced against the window. I was too relieved at being out of the field and being back in the world to care. Some MPs came from the guard shack with an M-16 and the crowd started to back off, but they still blocked the bus. The bus started to back up and the crowd started to throw rocks, hitting the bus. I felt like yelling out "Incoming!" A brown paper bag full of shit hit the window next to where my head was resting and sort of exploded. I could smell it immediately; it was human shit.

The bus turned around and went back to the processing center. We sat waiting in the bus at the processing center, where we had started. Someone said cabs were coming. I changed seats to get away from the smell. I wondered, as I sat there, why someone would throw a bag of human shit at our bus. I started to consider how you would go about filling a bag with human shit, and how you would transport it. These people must be pretty mad at us to go through all that. High fevers can make you have crazy thoughts. Even so, I didn't know why these people were so mad at us. I was twenty-one years old, I was sick, I was tired, and I just wanted to go home. It had been a long year. It had been four or five days since that last patrol, and I wondered, deep down, if they somehow had found out what I did that day.

A bunch of cabs showed up and we were piled into them, four or five to a cab. We had no luggage. We carried nothing but our Class A dress uniforms on our back, mine kind of stained. The officer in charge waited until all the cabs were filled and the bus was empty, and then sent each cab headed for a different gate at the same time. There was no way the protesters could stop all the cabs at different gates at the same time. It was hard to beat the Army when it came to field tactics. We got to the airport in our cabs with no problems. Nobody seemed to notice us when we got into the airport lobby. There were no protesters.

The airplane ride from Seattle to New York was quiet. My fever must have broken while I was asleep. I woke up as we landed and was feeling pretty good. I was with a guy named Vinny Natelle. Vinny and I had been together in basic and through Tiger Land. In New York City we decided to go out on the town. Back then the drinking age was eighteen and I had spent a lot of time there before I was drafted and sort of knew the hot spots.

We got in a cab and the cabbie asked us where we were coming from. We told him Vietnam and he stopped the cab, turned around in his seat, and said, "Oh, I have a couple of baby killers in my cab." I regret to this day that I didn't smash in his smiling face. I should have dragged him out of the cab and beat him senseless in the street. If it was a reaction he wanted, I should have given him one. Instead, Vinny and I just sort of laughed and looked at each other, not understanding the significance of the remark.

In the following months and years, this was pretty much the reaction of most people when I discussed my contribution to the war effort in Vietnam. I soon realized that discussing the war with anybody except another Vietnam Veteran was futile. I couldn't drag everybody that called me a baby killer out the middle of the street and smash there face in, even thought I wanted to.

Welcome Home

EPILOGUE

Only being in one war, I can not compare it to any others, but I'm sure for the infantry man, it's the same in all wars. It would be hard for me to believe that it was any easier or harder being in the infantry at the Battle of Gettysburg, Bunker Hill, or being in the army of Alexander the great. Hurt is hurt, blood is blood and dead is dead, it doesn't matter what century you are in.

After all the complaining and whining I do in this book, I bear no ill will towards the United States Army or the Government of the United States, we all did what we had to do. For my fellow Americans that supported Vietnam veterans over the years I give my thanks, for those who have chastised people like me for 30 years, I can only try to forgive.

From the day I'd DEROS out of Vietnam, June 3, 1969 until this very moment my entire life is viewed through a lens from the perspective of a grunt in Vietnam. Sometimes, it's a gift. Every morning I wake up, I smile just realizing I'm not in the jungle. I can never look at a glass of ice water or a clear summer night without incoming mortar fire and not consider it a gift from God

Sometimes, it's a curse. I still look for places to hide all day long in case I get ambushed, I walk into a room and I look around to see what I can use for a weapon.

It also showed me the face of evil, I don't talk about it much in the book, because for a grunt the evil is a given. We saw the atrocities committed on the people of South Vietnam by the Viet Cong and the North Vietnamese daily. It was common for us to spend a few days in a South Vietnamese village cleaning out the area of Viet Cong, when we packed up and were ready to move on young children would hold onto our legs begging us not to leave, because the Viet Cong would come back and burn their village. I can only imagine what must have happened, the wholesale slaughter and human tragedy when the United States packed up their bags for good and abandoned the South Vietnamese, somebody should feel some guilt for that.

There is a sign on the front of the Veterans Hospital that I go to that reads "The Price of Freedom is Shown Here." I think that sign sums up my feelings.

PART XLL

GLOSSARY OF MILITARY TERMS, ACRONYMS & SLANG

AIT—Advanced Infantry Training

AK-47—Soviet-manufactured semi-automatic assault rifle

AO—area of operation

APC—armed personnel carrier

ARVN—Army of the Republic of Vietnam; the South Vietnamese regular army

Arvin—soldier in the ARVN

AWOL—absent without leave

bandoliers—belts of machine gun ammunition

Bangalore Torpedoes—anti-personnel mine-clearing charges

C-4—plastic explosives

C-rations—combat rations; canned meals for use in the field

CA—combat assault

Camo Stick- face paint used for camouflage

Charlie—Viet Cong; the enemy

Chieu Hoi—clemency and financial aid program for Viet Cong and NVA soldiers who stopped fighting and returned to South Vietnamese government authority

Chinook—CH-47 cargo helicopter

CIB—combat infantry badge

CO—commanding officer

Cobra—AH-IG attack helicopter; also known as a gunship, armed with rockets and machine guns

CP—command post

CS—riot-control gas

Da Nang—capital of Quang Nam Province; second largest city in South Vietnam

DEROS—date of expected return from overseas

det-cord—detonating cord used with explosives

DMZ—demilitarized zone; the dividing line between North and South Vietnam established in 1954 at the Geneva Convention

dong—official currency of South Vietnam

dust-off—medical evacuation by helicopter

F-4—Phantom jet fighter-bombers

fatigues—standard combat uniform, green in color

fire base—temporary artillery encampment used for fire support of forward ground operations

firefight—a battle, or exchange of small arms fire with the enemy

flack jacket—heavy fiberglass-filled vest worn for protection from shrapnel

FO—forward observer; a person attached to a field unit to coordinate the placement of direct or indirect fire from ground, air, and naval forces

fragging—the assassination of an officer by his own troops, usually by a grenade

Freedom Bird—the plane that took soldiers from Vietnam back to "The World"

friendly fire—accidental attacks on U.S. or allied soldiers by other U.S. or allied soldiers

GI—government issue; an American soldier

gook—derogatory term for an Asian; derived from Korean slang for "person" and passed down by Korean war veterans

grenadier—infantry soldier who carries and throws grenades

grunt—infantryman

gunship—armed helicopter

heat tabs—flammable tablets used to heat C-rations

Ho Chi Minh Trail—elaborate system of mountain and jungle paths and trails used by North Vietnam to infiltrate troops and supplies into South Vietnam, Cambodia, and Laos

hooch—hut or simple dwelling

horn—radio microphone

hot—area under fire

HQ—headquarters

Huey—nickname for the UH-I series helicopter

I Corps—the northernmost military region in South Vietnam

in-country—Vietnam

Jody—the person who wins your lover or spouse while you are in Nam; from the marching song "Ain't no use in goin' home / Jody's got your girl and gone / Sound off...."

lager—night defensive perimeter (pronounced lä' ger); from Afrikaans, meaning a camp defended by a circular formation of wagons

LBJ—Long Binh Jail; a military stockade on Long Binh post

Leavenworth, Fort—home of U.S. military prison, in Kansas

lifer—career military man

LP—listening post

LZ—landing zone

M-I4—wood-stock rifle used in early portion of Vietnam conflict

M-I6—standard U.S. military rifle

M-60—standard lightweight machine gun used by U.S. forces in Vietnam

M-79—U.S. military handheld grenade launcher

mad minute—weapons free-fire practice and test session

mama san—pidgin used by American servicemen for older Vietnamese woman

medivac—medical evacuation from the field by helicopter

Minigun—electronically controlled, rapid-firing machine gun; most often mounted on aircraft to be used against targets on the ground

mortar—muzzle-loading cannon

MOS—Military Occupational Specialty

MP—military police

MPC—Military Payment Currency; U.S. Army scrip

Nam—Vietnam

napalm—jellied petroleum substance that burned fiercely; used as a weapon against personnel

NCO—noncommissioned officer

NVA—North Vietnamese Army

OJT—on-the-job training

OP—observation post

P-38—tiny collapsible can opener

perimeter—outer limits of a military position; the area beyond the perimeter belongs to the enemy

PF—Popular Forces; South Vietnamese, National Guard–type units

PFC—private first class

platoon—subdivision of a company-sized military unit, normally consisting of two or more squads or sections

point—forward man or element on a combat patrol

pop smoke—ignite a smoke grenade to signal an aircraft

POW—prisoner of war

PP—permanent point

PRC-25—Portable Radio Communications, Model 25; backpacked FM receiver-transmitter used for short-distance communications

R&R—rest and recreation; a three- to seven-day vacation from the war

REMF—rear-echelon mother fucker

RHIP—rank has its privileges

RPG—rocket-propelled grenade

rucksack—backpack issued to infantry in Vietnam

short-timer—soldier nearing the end of his tour in Vietnam

shrapnel—pieces of metal sent flying by an explosion

SKS—Simonov 7.62 mm semi-automatic carbine

slant—derogatory term for a Vietnamese person

slick—UH-I helicopter used for transporting troops in tactical air assault operations

smoke grenade—grenade that released brightly colored smoke; used for signaling

Special Forces—elite U.S. Army troops who played a key role in counterinsurgency operations during the Vietnam War. The Army of the Republic of Vietnam also had Special Forces teams.

spider hole—camouflaged enemy foxhole

squad—small military unit consisting of less than ten men

stand-down—infantry unit's return from the bush to base camp for refitting and training; later, a unit being withdrawn from Vietnam and redeployed to the U.S.

starlight scope—image intensifier using reflected light to identify targets at night

Tiger Land—jungle infantry training camp at Fort Polk, Louisiana, specially designed for ground troops assigned to Vietnam

tracer—round of ammunition chemically treated to glow or give off smoke so that its flight can be followed

tracks—any vehicles that move on tracks rather than wheels

triage—procedure for deciding the order in which to treat casualties

trip flare—ground flare triggered by a trip wire used to signal and illuminate the approach of an enemy at night

VC—Viet Cong; the National Liberation Front

Viet Cong—Communist-led forces fighting the South Vietnamese government

Wall, The—the Vietnam Veterans Memorial Wall in Washington, D.C.

web gear—canvas belt and shoulder straps for packing equipment and ammunition on infantry operations

World, the—the United States

Zippo units—napalm flame throwers

BOOK ORDER FORM

Give the gift of *"Alone in Vietnam"*

Yes, I want _____copies of *"Alone in Vietnam"* for $16 each plus $3.00 for shipping for a total of $19.00 per copy

<u>SEE OUR WEB PAGE AT:</u>
http://www.independentpublisher-us.com:80/alonein-vietnam.htm

My check or money order for $_____ is enclosed

Name_____

Organization_____

Address_____

City/State/zip_____ e-mail_____

M.C./VISA/AE ._____.Card #_____

Expiration date_____

Signature_____

Phone orders
Call one 1-866-766-2253
<u>Make your check payable and return to:</u>

Red Dog Books
PO box 1242
Glastonbury, CT 06033

Attn: corporations, universities, colleges, and professional organizations: quantity discounts are available on bulk purchases of this book for educational, purposes, or as premiums for increasing magazine subscriptions or renewals, special books or book and Serbs can also be created to fit specific needs. For information, please contact my publishing company, **Red Dog Books, P.O. Box 1242, Glastonbury, CT 06033 or call 1-866-766-2253.**

E-mail <u>424219@comcast.net</u>

4701607R0